JAM!

Work Hard Rock Harder

JAM!

aMP YOUR TeaM, ROCK YOUR BUSINeSS

JeFF CarLiSi & Dan LiPSON

WITH JaY BUSBee

JOSSEY-BASS
A Wiley Imprint
www.josseybass.com

Published by Jossey-Bass
A Wiley Imprint
989 Market Street, San Francisco, CA 94103-1741—www.josseybass.com

Jossey-Bass books and products are available through most bookstores.
To contact Jossey-Bass directly call our Customer Care Department within the
U.S. at 800-956-7739, outside the U.S. at 317-572-3986, or fax 317-572-4002.

Jossey-Bass also publishes its books in a variety of electronic formats. Some content
that appears in print may not be available in electronic books.

Library of Congress Cataloging-in-Publication Data

Carlisi, Jeff.
    Jam! : amp your team, rock your business / Jeff Carlisi, Dan Lipson,
with Jay Busbee.—1st ed.
        p.   cm.
    Includes bibliographical references and index.
    ISBN 978-0-470-44652-2 (cloth)
        1. Rock music—Vocational guidance.   I. Lipson, Dan, 1957–
II. Busbee, Jay.   III. Title.
ML3795.C29   2009
781.66023′73—dc22

                                                                      2009004392
FIRST EDITION
HB Printing   10 9 8 7 6 5 4 3 2 1

Contents

Contents

Introduction

Hello, Cleveland! (Or wherever you are as you read these words.)

I'm Jeff Carlisi. For more than twenty years, I played in the band 38 Special. I toured the world, sold millions of albums, wrote and recorded a bunch of hits, and performed before millions of fans. Along the way, I learned that success doesn't come from talent or drive alone; you've got to think like a professional from the moment you strum your first note. And so once I left 38 and entered the business world, I realized I was in familiar territory.

Although you wouldn't expect it, the legendary business teams that created and lead Microsoft, Disney, and Starbucks have much in common with the Rolling Stones and U2. Each group consists of extraordinary individuals who achieve greatness because of the players they assembled and how well that team functions day after day, year after year. Together the team exceeds the sum of its parts, going further together than any individual could go alone.

Sure, it's tough to imagine any worlds more different from those of button-down business and crank-it-up rock'n'roll. But look past the surface. Both have more than their share of egos and "rock stars." Both require the right mix of marquee names and supporting cast. And both can suffer more from success than they can from failure.

Like a business, a successful rock band is made up of both visionaries and devoted followers, leaders and team players. But the band achieves success only when the entire group is pulling in the same direction. When each member understands the part he or she must play within the group, contributing creatively and playing to his or her strengths, that's when the hits start coming.

My business partner and cowriter, Dan Lipson, and I have plenty of experience in both the music and business worlds. Since leaving 38, I joined with Dan to form Camp Jam Inc., an organization that promotes team building and business development through rock'n'roll. At corporate retreats and in team-building exercises, the Camp Jam faculty transforms business colleagues into instant rock 'n' roll bands, forming bonds that last long after the ears stop ringing.

In *Jam!* I give you everything from great rock stories—like the tale of the architect who became a guitar hero and the multimillion-selling track that almost never was—and Dan offers up practical, hands-on business advice in how to run your company and your career as if you're playing before a packed house.

Each chapter of *Jam!* examines a key moment in the development of a band—formation, early success, internal crises, and so forth—and demonstrates how you can use those lessons to crank your own business to eleven. You'll also see how the world's best-known bands and singers triumphed over their own challenges, offering useful lessons for everyone in the business world.

You'll read insights from musicians who have played in some of the world's best-known bands, including the Rolling Stones and the Eagles, and backed superstars like Billy Joel, Eric Clapton, Keith Richards, Ozzy Osbourne, Roger Daltrey, Don Henley, and Sheryl Crow. You've seen these people onstage, bought their CDs, listened to their music on your way to work. Why not learn a little something from them to take in the door with you?

Finally, in each chapter, Dan and I offer a concluding Verse, Chorus, and Solo, takeaways for both you and your team. "Verse" recaps the main message of the chapter, "Chorus" gives your team a way to approach the chapter's themes, and "Solo" gives you the opportunity to take the chapter's elements in your own direction. Like the song that sticks in your head for days afterward, we hope you'll leave each chapter of *Jam!* with a little melody to carry into your office the next day.

And by the end of the book, you'll live by our mantra: *Work hard. Rock harder.*

Showtime is here. The house lights are down. The crowd is chanting your name. Ready to take the stage?

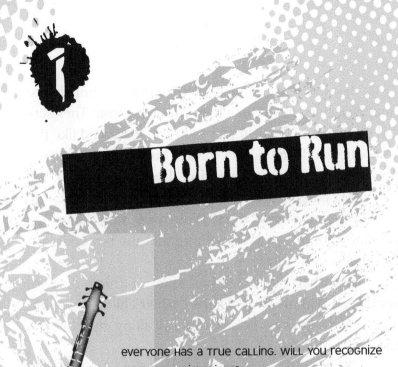

Born to Run

everyone has a true calling. will you recognize yours when it's time?

Musical geniuses like Mozart and Hendrix began playing, even composing, almost before they could walk. I wasn't quite so gifted. I was just a normal kid growing up in Jacksonville, Florida, in the late 1950s and early 1960s. Music wasn't that much of a draw to me, not when there were sports and playing to be done. The first song I remember liking was Johnny Horton's "The Battle of New Orleans," but even then, it wasn't an "aha" moment. I just liked the groove.

Somewhere around my tenth birthday, though, my parents decided it was time to get me into music. They settled on piano; my cousin played it, and it seemed like the best option at the time. They tracked down a piano teacher, who offered up some sage advice: "Don't buy a piano."

My parents were confused. Why not buy a piano? This was an *investment,* right? Why throw money away on a rental when this was something that the boy could do for the rest of his life?

But that piano teacher knew a thing or two. She'd seen parents with visions of their children playing standing-room-only recitals, while all along, the children had different ideas.

"If the child is interested in the piano," the teacher said, "there's always time to buy the piano. But if the child isn't interested in the piano, you're stuck with a very expensive piece of firewood."

"So what are our options?" my parents asked. The piano teacher gave an answer that makes me cringe to this day: "You can rent an accordion from me."

So there it was. Technically the first instrument I ever learned to play was an accordion with that droning, bleating tone.

The lessons I took largely consisted of scales and exercises, running do-re-mi up and down the accordion's keyboard. I did well enough at it, I suppose, but my heart wasn't in it. I was ten years old, trying to play an instrument that's not exactly the most glamorous or easy to play.

What made matters worse, from a teaching perspective, was that I discovered I could play songs by ear.

I'd be sitting at home watching cartoons, and I'd start to pick the theme songs out on the accordion. I could listen to, say, the theme from *Popeye* and play, "I'm Popeye the sailor man," with only a little bit of trial-and-error.

This was a revelation to me, and one that anyone who has been involved in any kind of creative endeavor, be it designing Web sites or devising sales techniques, can intuitively understand. There's a proper way to do things, a prescribed path. It's why everything from roads to baseball fields to sheet music has boundary lines. But the true discoveries come when you cross those lines and veer off into the unknown.

Of course, if you do veer off the beaten path, be prepared for some unpleasantness when you return. Each week I'd return to practice, and my teacher would ask me how I was doing with my scales. "The scales are fine," I'd say, "but listen to this!" And I'd play her the *Popeye* theme, and she'd tell me to knock it off and get back to "serious" music.

Nothing against my poor accordion teacher, but after just a few weeks of that, I'd had enough and walked away.

Even all these years later, I do wonder what would have happened if I'd played piano rather than accordion. I might have followed through with my lessons, learned my scales, and become something of a decent player. To this day, I wish I played more piano.

Parents often wrestle with this idea of how to get their kid into music. The kid sees his favorite bands onstage or plays the Guitar Hero video game, and obviously, he (or she, of course) wants to be a rock star.

He wants to stand onstage in front of thousands of fans, cranking out songs at ear-bleeding volume. He wants it so badly that his parents figure it can't be good for him. Like candy and cartoons, if he wants it that much, there must be something wrong with it.

So they try to steer him toward what they think is the "healthier" side of music, starting small with an acoustic guitar. But it's tougher to play, it doesn't sound as cool, and most important, it's nowhere near as loud. Still, there's a perception that you have to learn the basics on an acoustic guitar before you can rock out with an electric one.

Nonsense. If the kid wants the flaming red guitar, and not getting it means the kid's not going to be playing music, by all means, get the kid a flaming red guitar. You never know how much further someone will go doing something he wants to do rather than something he has to do.

If you're a manager, take a close look at the people under your control. I certainly don't mean to equate them with children, but there's a lesson to be learned from the flaming red guitar. Chances are that your employees aren't going to refuse a new project assignment from you outright. (If they are, you've got deeper problems; we'll discuss those sorts of things when we get to Chapter Seven on band strife.)

However, just because you've sent them to a particular conference or encouraged them to take a particular skills course doesn't mean they're going to like it or get anything out of it. Know your people; know their strengths. Don't send the homebodies on the road when you can send the smooth talkers. Otherwise they'll end up like the kids who don't get the electric guitars: resentful, then bored, then uninterested. But while the kid without the guitar can't walk out the door and find a new set of parents who'll give him what he wants, an employee who doesn't feel challenged or interested might not be an employee for much longer. And it might not be your choice when this employee decides to go.

The Moment It All Clicked

My story doesn't end with me walking away from the accordion, of course.

For me, as for so many of my peers, the defining moment of my musical life was seeing the Beatles appear on the *Ed Sullivan Show*. Over the course of three Sundays in February 1964, the Beatles were beamed into millions of American living rooms and changed the course of music history forever. They played songs that we all know by heart now, but back then nobody had ever heard anything like "I Want to Hold Your Hand," "All My Loving," and "I Saw Her Standing There."

I saw the Beatles, and that was it. I was hooked, and there was nothing else I could imagine myself doing again. The Beatles influenced so many people in so many ways; some liked the long hair, some liked the cool suits, some liked the hundreds of screaming fans.

For me, it was the electric guitar.

There was something to that look, that style that John Lennon and George Harrison had, the way their guitars cut through everything around them. I couldn't explain it then, and I'm not sure I can explain it now. But something in the way they looked onstage touched me on a deep level, and I knew I had to be a part of that. After that night, I talked my father into getting me a guitar, and never looked back.

There's a school of thought that holds that rock'n' roll is all about "feel"—that traditional musical elements like notation and sheet music have no place when you're getting up in front of a crowd to rock. And that's true to a certain extent. We're not the symphony; our music breathes and can change from night to night.

However, long before you can get up there in front of the crowd, you've got to put in the time with those traditional musical elements. Guitarists call it "woodshedding," as in "going out to the woodshed to practice." You spend the downtime practicing so that you can spend the uptime playing.

The great guitarist Larry Carlton once told me that his philosophy toward the guitar was simple: "Play what you love, but practice what you must." In other words, you want to play rock guitar? Great! But make sure you practice the basic fundamentals, as well as jazz, country, and blues. When you're young, it's a delicate balance of keeping yourself interested in the instrument while building a foundation of musical knowledge.

When I was in seventh grade, I was fortunate enough to find a teacher who helped me bridge the gap between playing what I wanted and learning what I needed. And as it turned out, he was only two years older than me. Terry Cosgrove was a guitar teacher ahead of his time, one who showed me only what I needed to get up to speed and play some simple rock riffs. He gave me the gratification of playing the riff to a song I could hear on the radio. Maybe I didn't fully grasp how one riff related to another, but early on, I didn't need to. Just developing the love affair with the guitar was enough.

Think about what put you where you are in your career. Was it a family business? Did you follow a mentor? Did you just happen to answer the right job posting? For any job, dozens of elements have to come together at exactly the right time for you to be where you are right now.

Think back to everything that had to fall in place. A chance meeting at a cocktail party. One more phone call to a prospective client. One more résumé sent out. When you look at it that way, it's fairly amazing that you are where you are. Would I still be where I am if I hadn't seen that *Ed Sullivan Show?* Possibly. But possibly not. Would you still be where you are if you hadn't had that one moment of opportunity?

The obvious next step, then, is to take that opportunity and build on it. Put yourself in a position for opportunities to arrive, and you'll be amazed at the doors that can open.

For me, the door was labeled "Marshmallow Steamshovel."

The Best Band Names in the World

When I was growing up, everybody around me either played in a band or wanted to. Those of us lucky to be playing in bands tended to jump ship pretty frequently, going from band to band every year. It wasn't like a summer romance; it was much more serious than that. In my early teens, I joined some bands that were unforgettable, if only for the names:

The Summer Sons. My first band. My guitar teacher invited me to join him in this one. We'd play British Invasion songs, and tunes like Sam the Sham and the Pharaohs' "Woolly Bully." (Years later, I got to play "Woolly Bully" alongside Sam the Sham himself. If someone had told me in 1965 that I'd be doing that thirty years later, I can't imagine how I would have reacted.)

Marshmallow Steamshovel. By now we'd started incorporating a little bit of soul into our repertoire, playing songs from Motown and Memphis. We were still trying to imitate the Beatles—everybody was at that point—and since they'd released *Sergeant Pepper's Lonely Hearts Club Band,* we rented some fancy marching-band costumes to try to tap into their look. We ended up looking more like Paul Revere and the Raiders—a little odd and out of place in the gyms and recreation centers where we played.

Doomsday Refreshment Committee. Still a cool name for a band, if you ask me. Our drum head featured the old Kool-Aid Man pitcher with a mushroom cloud coming out of the top of his head! Doomsday was the time I started thinking of myself as a real guitarist, for reasons I'll explain in a moment.

Sweet Rooster. This was band in which I started playing with Donnie Van Zant and Ken Lyons, two of my future bandmates in 38. I didn't know it at the time, but I'd be spending most of the next twenty-five years with them.

What do all four of these bands have in common besides the strange names? In all four, I was learning not just the music but the lifestyle of the musician. That meant learning to play well as part of a larger group. This is a major theme of this book, one we'll return to many times, and here's where it starts.

If you can't jell with your bandmates almost from the start, it's going to be a long, hard road for you, and one that might end sooner than you expect. (Ask Pete Best about that. Pete was a drummer who didn't fit in so well with the other three members of his group. They cut him loose, and while he struggled with a solo career, they went on to become the Beatles.)

Working in small groups can be the bane of your workday existence. You've got one person who wants to dominate, one who wants to do nothing but cruise on the rest of the group's efforts, one who goes along to get along. We'll go into more detail about small-group interrelations in later chapters, but for now, the focus should be on yourself. Every time you find yourself part of a new team, you should be asking yourself these questions:

🎸 What's my role in this group?

🎸 What do I bring to the group that no one else can?

🎸 How am I contributing to (or detracting from) the success of the group?

🎸 How much responsibility will I have in keeping the group afloat?

🎸 Which of my teammates can I learn from, and what can I learn?

This kind of self-examination will help you become a better group member much faster than if you just show up with your instrument and expect to join the band. Although we were in our early teens at this time, we were already working our way through these kinds of tough questions. Some of us answered the right way and ended up making a career of all this; others decided that they didn't like the answers and moved on to other pursuits. No harm in that, certainly. It's far better to find out too early what you're suited for than too late.

So let's take a closer look at how I answered the questions above:

• *What's my role in this group?* Initially I was the rhythm guitarist. That's the guy who plays the chords in the background, keeping the song moving while the lead guitarist steps to the front for the solos. It was an important apprenticeship, watching how the group worked together all around me.

- *What do I bring to the group that no one else can?* In my earliest groups, there wasn't much I could do that a bunch of other guys couldn't. But I did have a cool guitar—a 1967 Fender Telecaster Custom—and a willingness to try out new ideas and work with my bandmates. I also had a horrible little mustache, but the less said about that, the better.

- *How am I contributing to (or detracting from) the success of the group?* When you're young and in a band, it's not just about what goes on onstage. You've got to handle all sides of the process, from booking dates to publicizing concerts to hauling equipment to (we hoped) getting paid and handling the money. I was always willing to jump in and take on more than my share of those responsibilities in order to do what I could to keep the group moving forward.

- *How much responsibility will I have in keeping the group afloat?* Since most of these early groups didn't last more than a summer, I guess you'd think I didn't have much success, right? And you'd be correct—sort of. Every musician's early bands are like training wheels, meant to be discarded as you move up to higher speeds. Sure, Keith Richards and Mick Jagger have known each other since elementary school, but they're the exception rather than the rule. Figure out how much work you'll need to put in versus how much value you'll get out, and then you can decide how well your group is faring.

- *Which of my teammates can I learn from, and what can I learn?* Now we're getting into the heart of it all. You can, of course, learn something from anybody, even if it's what not to do in a certain situation. But what propels you forward is when you learn from those who have been where you are and have already stepped ahead. For me, the Doomsday Refreshment Committee, a tiny band, was the launching pad for a career that put me in front of sold-out stadiums. And it was all because of one guy who played me the blues.

Verse

Nobody this side of Mozart is born a musician. But almost anyone can practice into musical competence. It's the same way with your business: figure out what your particular calling is, and work your way toward that.

Chorus

When you're part of a group, you've got to ask yourself some questions to make sure you're being the best teammate you can possibly be: What's my role in this group? What do I bring to the group that no one else can? How am I contributing to (or detracting from) the success of the group? How much responsibility will I have in keeping the group afloat? Which of my teammates can I learn from, and what can I learn? Thinking in global terms like this, looking beyond your group's to-do list, will help your group focus more on what needs to be done rather than how it's going to get done.

Solo

Examine your own career. What's the most fascinating part to you, and what part do you wish you could put behind you once and for all? If you were told to take one element of your career and do only that element and you'd get all the benefits you're receiving right now, what element would that be?

Dream On

DREAMING OF SUCCESS IS A LOT MORE FUN THAN WORKING FOR IT. BUT IF YOU WANT TO HIT THE TOP OF THE CHARTS, YOU HAVE TO PUT IN THE HARD WORK LONG BEFORE THE CROWDS SHOW UP.

If you've ever spent any time hunting for a job—or, for that matter, a girlfriend or boyfriend—you have an idea of the trickiness involved in joining a new band. A potential partnership can go wrong in an infinite number of ways: you want them more than they want you, you've got concerns about control or potential, you're wondering whether everyone's headed in the same direction.

Once you hit a certain age, finding that perfect match, whether a band, a job, or a significant other, becomes considerably more difficult as everyone's preferences start locking in. But early on, the world is wide open before you. When I was in high school, I joined a different band every year. It wasn't like a summer romance; it ran much deeper than that.

Somewhere along the line, though, I realized I hadn't yet begun to understand what it really meant to be a musician. That moment came when I met a guy named Robert Corchran. The keyboard player for the notorious Doomsday Refreshment Committee, Robert was four years older than I was—which in those high school days meant he qualified as a wise elder. And he played the role well, introducing me and my bandmates to that mysteriously enticing form of music known the world over as the blues.

Sure, we'd heard the blues before. We'd listened to Cream and Hendrix and the bluesier sides of the Rolling Stones. But that was the blues reflected—in some cases, sent all the way across the Atlantic, repackaged, and brought back to us by kids not much older than we were. They weren't bluesmen any more than I was a rock god.

Still, they'd tapped into something primal, something that I didn't yet know existed. Without going too deep into musical theory, the blues gets its name from the "blue notes," the slightly sharped or flattened versions of major-scale notes. (The best-known major scale is C major, which consists of all the white keys on the piano.) These blue notes give music a slightly unsettled, off-center feel—something you can't pinpoint but can understand in your heart and soul. They're the musical version of an emotional state. They're also the map to an entirely new continent that every guitarist must someday explore.

We'd heard songs like Cream's "Crossroads" and the Rolling Stones' "Love in Vain," but we'd never heard the original versions of these songs. We'd never heard B.B. King, Albert King, Muddy Waters, or any of the other old blues masters from whom all these amazing sounds and songs derived. Listening to those scratchy old songs was like going into an attic and finding a masterpiece hidden under dusty cloth. It had been there all along; I just wasn't yet ready to find it.

Once I began listening to the blues and realized I was part of a larger spectrum of music, things really opened up for me. That kicked it up a notch. I felt that I was becoming a guitar player, that the blues had broadened the scope of my instrument.

Think about your own industry. There are "bluesmen" and "blueswomen" who paved the way for you and your company to be where you are right now, pioneers whose work was so groundbreaking that it's literally impossible to imagine how your industry could exist without them. And as a result, it's easy now to take their contributions for granted. In music, we're five or six generations past the earliest blues pioneers, and there are entire generations of fans who've never heard a song by Robert Johnson, the 1930s Mississippi bluesman who inspired all of rock 'n' roll.

Along the same lines, think about the most significant advances in business. Everything from mass production to hub-and-spoke distribution is so deeply ingrained in our business culture that we don't even consider their influence any longer. And yet there was a time when these innovations didn't exist; there were leaders and visionaries who had to imagine and dream big.

Look at the foundations of your own industry, whether through the biographies of its founders or—if you happen to be in a younger field—through discussion with some of the wise elders. Then take one step back from there. What gap did these men and women see that needed to be filled? What problem did they identify as demanding a solution? What ideas did they come up with before devising the one that hit? The blues is a stew of everything from old spiritual hymns to field hollers to storytelling ballads. Individually these musical forms express different ideas and emotions; together they tap into something deeper than any could do alone.

What you'll learn by doing a similar excavation of your own industry's history is why certain approaches work in your industry and others don't. Obviously an industry dominated by human contact demands different approaches from one based on technology.

You don't need to reinvent the wheel; just try to figure out why it got invented in the first place. Think about it in terms of your senses. Musicians onstage use almost all the five senses, and you too can expand your range of awareness of your own situation:

- Observe what's different about your job and your career now than it was five, ten, twenty, or fifty years ago. Observing the path and speed of change in history can help you prepare for the inevitable changes coming down the road.
- Listen to what others are saying about your company and your industry. Pay attention to trade reports, message boards, and your customers.

If everybody's saying something different, you can make your own call, but if everybody's saying the same thing, pay attention.

🎸 Get a sense of your own place within your company. How prized is the work you do? How can you work to increase your own prestige and value? How can you maintain and strengthen your position within your company?

Open Your Eyes

My senior year of high school, I joined my fourth and final high school band, Sweet Rooster. We were doing the usual circuit of parties, but none of us knew at the time that this band was the roots of a platinum seller. Sweet Rooster was where I began playing with Donnie Van Zant, who would eventually become my bandmate for so many years.

The blues introduced me to a completely different range of music than I'd been listening to. Absorbing that music, learning from it, and hearing how those musicians tackled challenges in a different way than I would have was a completely new level of schooling for me.

Thing is, I wasn't yet done with the traditional form of schooling. As much as I loved the idea of playing music, I had no illusions. Making a living in music is phenomenally tough, and I didn't want to put myself in a dead-end situation by closing off all my options. Playing music was fun, sure, but being an architect—now, that was a job I could get behind. That was a job worth going to college for, and that's what I did.

You don't have to dig too deep to see the similarities between music and architecture; both demand creation and imagination, as well as a healthy grasp of fundamentals. Maybe that's why I could envision myself as an architect; I was channeling my creative energies into the nearest available economically viable outlet. I moved north from Jacksonville to Atlanta to begin classes at Georgia Tech, figuring that my musical days were going to be confined to weekend afternoons with the guys.

"We all have a passion in ourselves, and for me that passion is music. . . . If you have passion for your art, for your work, other people are going to see that and feed off of it."
—DON FELDER, FORMER GUITARIST, THE EAGLES

Music wasn't ready to let me go, though, and I couldn't help paying attention to all the music going on around me in Atlanta. It was country music! For a guy who'd been raised on rock, the r&b of Stax Records and Motown, and later the blues, country was still undiscovered territory. But in Atlanta, everyone was playing it, and playing it really well.

I was soaking everything up back then, and country music worked its way right into my soul alongside blues. I didn't have the faintest idea who the pioneers of country music were, but I knew that the pedal steel guitar—a sit-down instrument that combines guitar necks and pedals to make soaring, soulful chords—made a sound I'd heard nowhere else. I used to go to a little music store in Smyrna, Georgia, called the Music Mart, and the guys there could play pedal steel sweetly enough to make you cry, hot enough to burn the walls. They were incredible, and I knew I had to be a part of that. I bought a pedal steel of my own and started playing this amazing new (to me) style of music. It would serve me well for years to come. (I actually got an offer to join the band of a young singer by the name of Barbara Mandrell. I was flattered, but I passed. Good thing, too, because I was nowhere near ready to be a professional musician.)

What I was doing is developing my signature sound. And here's how you can do the exact same thing.

The Signature Sound

Imagine your favorite musicians all lined up on-stage somewhere: Keith Richards, Bono, Eddie Van Halen, George Harrison, and so many others. Now, imagine they all play the same song—"Happy Birthday," "Mary Had a Little Lamb," "Jingle Bells," whatever. You're going to be able to tell in an instant that each version of the song sounds dramatically different; one might be in-your-face distortion, while another is smooth, silky, and jazz tinged. One might be played at breakneck speed, another at a slow, languid bluesy pace. And if your ear is attuned enough, you might even be able to tell who's doing the playing. No two guitarists sound exactly alike. Every musician is the sum total of his or her influences, combined with individual initiative, drive, and creativity. Keith Richards couldn't sound like Eddie Van Halen if he tried, and vice versa.

You too are the sum of your influences. And while a father's or mother's lessons or a college professor's wisdom may not end up on anybody's iPod, they're nonetheless an exceptional resource for you to determine how you're going to approach your own challenges. Think back to some of the earliest professional advice you received. Does it still hold true? If you're like most other people, the further you go in your career, the more you realize what an influence a strong mentor can have on you.

And your signature sound? Well, that's for you to determine, but it's a combination of comfort zone and confidence. Do you stride into a crisis, take charge, bark out orders, and get people to snap right in line? Or are you a quiet decider, sitting back and contemplating all possible options before taking action? Do you build consensus, or do you make unilateral decisions? Once you can determine your own signature sound, you can shape it, refine it, and help build confidence across your organization.

How does a signature sound build confidence? Simple. You know that when you buy, say, a new album by Aerosmith, you're not going to get a CD of Gregorian chants or hip-hop tracks. You're going to get straight-ahead rock 'n' roll from the best in the business. Similarly, by being consistent (but not necessarily predictable), you assure your coworkers and subordinates that they can know what to expect from you in times of calm and in times of crisis. And take it from someone who has seen plenty of diva behavior on the road: in the long run, reliability is worth far more than occasional sparks of genius.

Think of your signature sound as a radio. You've got various influences pouring in, and from the other side—the broadcasting side—out comes your own particular sound. You have no idea where it's going to go, you have no idea who your own sound will in turn influence, but it's yours and nobody else's.

Part of the way you develop a signature sound is by understanding what you don't do well, in addition to having a firm grasp on your expertise. To put it in purely musical terms, I recommend that anyone trying to learn an instrument listen to everything they can get their hands on. They don't have to like it. In fact, there may be music out there that they flat-out loathe. But they won't know that until they sit down with that music, pull it apart, understand its components, understand what makes it different from any other song ever written. They can learn something from any song, whether it's a classic or a here-today and gone-later-today disposable pop band. (Perhaps you'll learn not to slavishly follow trends, but that's a lesson worth learning.)

The same rules apply in business. Your own signature sound may be more of a signature style—a way of approaching everything from managerial challenges to company outings—and you develop that in much the same way that a guitarist makes his instrument his own.

• *Learn everything there is to know about your own business.* Learn your industry's history to understand the challenges it has faced and how the greatest minds in the industry overcame them. The cell phone industry, for example, met the challenge of saturation by looking in new directions: adding more features to the average cell phone, enforcing disposability of phones, and cutting the cost of a new phone while locking in customers with long-term contracts. You'd be hard pressed to find someone without a cell phone now. You'd have almost the same challenge finding someone whose phone doesn't have games, texting, e-mail, or other nonphone features. Understand how, in this case, lateral thinking opened new doors people didn't even know existed.

• *Cross the genre lines.* Just as a rock guitarist can learn plenty from listening to country, jazz, and funk, so too can you learn plenty from observing businesses that don't seem anywhere close to your own. In need of some understanding of the complexities of inventory control? See how everyone from tire dealers to cookie bakers handles inventory. Interested in learning more about cutting shipping costs? Observe the shipping techniques of everyone from Wal-Mart to the stay-at-home mom creating embroidered baby clothing. There's something you can learn from every business, some tip that you can add to your own arsenal. For a guitarist, it might be a genre-bending riff; for you, it might be a cross-industry insight.

• *Look for the roadblocks beyond your headlights.* Start to project out where future challenges may lie—and understand that they don't always come from the direction you'd expect. For instance, Blockbuster might have thought that its greatest competition came from other forms of entertainment, like movies and television. But it turns out that its greatest competition was not product or even pricing but distribution: the way NetFlix began delivering DVDs straight to customers' doors completely revamped Blockbuster's way of doing business. We'll discuss in more detail later keeping yourself in tune with popular trends without being a slave to them.

The main thing to remember is not to get tunnel vision. I tell younger guitarists this all the time: it's okay if you want to absorb the influence of Hendrix or Kurt Cobain; just make sure you listen to *more* than Hendrix or Cobain. Those guys didn't restrict themselves to one form of music, and nobody else should either.

In the same way, you can get hung up following one career path, one style of management, one way of looking at your industry. Having vision and ambition is fine, but it shouldn't prevent you from remaining open to other ideas, other potential influences. In the earlier stages of your professional development, these influences shape you; as you move onward, the influences are like spices, adding a new tinge or taste to what you've already got cooking.

The Local Boys Make Good

Even while I was in college, I was constantly playing in bands, mostly as a release and a way to get out and see a different side of Atlanta. At the same time, some guys I'd grown up admiring in Jacksonville had also made the journey up Interstate 75 to Atlanta. They were starting to draw a bit of interest for their music, even if nobody quite knew how to pronounce their name: Lynyrd Skynyrd.

In 1971, Skynyrd was playing at some pretty rough clubs, the kind where you look back and think, *How did I get out of there alive?* But they were tearing up the music scene, and people were starting to pay attention. I remember several of my friends telling me I needed to hear this new band from Jacksonville; I laughed, because I'd been hearing them for years before anyone else.

Lynyrd Skynyrd was at the forefront of a new wave of Southern rock out of Atlanta that included musicians like the Atlanta Rhythm Section, Eric Quincy Tate, and Mose Jones. Like Athens, Georgia, a decade later and Seattle two decades on, Atlanta was fermenting its own brew of rock music, the bands all observing and learning from one another to create a new genre almost out of thin air.

One night, Al Kooper, the famous producer and session man (he's the guy playing the organ on Bob

Dylan's "Like a Rolling Stone"), happened to be in town and caught Skynyrd live. He was blown away, the same way everyone who saw Skynyrd in those days was, and he signed them to MCA's Sounds of the South record label. And from there, they were off and running.

It was an exciting time to be a musician, even one on the sidelines like I was. I remember watching Skynyrd play and record and thinking, "This is amazing. There's really something special going on here." And those can be dangerous thoughts if you're a kid on his way through college but with an uncertain future. I was seeing friends make it, or at least potentially make it, in music. I had every chance to bail out of school and try to make a go of it in music. Maybe I would have been a success. Maybe not. But I certainly wouldn't have had the safety net that I got from sticking with school.

I had some people looking out for me, though. Skynyrd's lead singer was Ronnie Van Zant, older brother of Donnie, my bandmate in Sweet Rooster. If anybody should have told me to take a run at that musical brass ring, it should have been him. But when Kooper offered me a spot in his band Blues Project, Ronnie gave me the exact opposite advice that you'd expect. "Stay in school," he told me. "Music will be there when you get out."

It was a tough thing to hear, but a good lesson to learn. Too many times, we get seduced by something that sounds too good to be true. More to the point, we get a chance to live out a dream, but we're not yet ready to take that leap. I was a single guy with no obligations, nothing standing in my way. And even so, I had to ask myself a few hard questions, the kinds of things you should ask yourself any time you stand on the edge of a major new endeavor:

- *What am I walking away from, and what am I walking toward?* "I want to join a rock band" has to be one of the top dreams of any teenager. But just wanting isn't enough. You've got to know exactly what you'll be getting yourself into and exactly what you're giving up. Staying in school to be an architect wasn't exactly the glamorous route when compared to the dream of being a rock star. But as we'll see in later chapters, the dreamy life was just that—a dream—for many years.

- *How much of my future depends on me, and how much on other people?* This is a key question, and one that we'll explore in greater detail later. You've got to know how much of your future is in your own control. For me, I'd practiced to get my skills to a certain point, but at that point, I'd need bandmates equally dedicated in order to take the next step upward. We've all been in situations where we've worked in a group and one of our members wouldn't shoulder his or her own weight. Staying in school, I was the master of my own destiny; joining the rock band put my fate in others' hands.

- *What if I fail?* It's not pleasant to think about, but every new endeavor is filled with risk. It's like the old line about gambling: never play with more than you can afford to lose. For me, I was looking at giving up on a college degree and walking away from a reliable, if not guaranteed, future. Your level of risk may be much higher than a college kid's, and it's something you've got to consider if you're going to take that leap.

- *What if I succeed?* It's said that if you want to make someone truly miserable, give them their heart's desire. On first glance, that seems absurd. Aren't we always chasing our own dreams? But as we'll see in later chapters, sometimes getting exactly what you want is the worst thing that could possibly happen, particularly if you haven't planned for it.

As it turned out, I put my musical dreams on hold, but only for a bit. I graduated from college in 1974, not the best time to be looking for a job. The economy was in horrible shape, oil embargoes were dominating the headlines, and nobody was building anything, which meant there wasn't a lot of opportunity for a newly graduated architect.

So I went back to Jacksonville, where they were still playing music.

Verse

Sometimes the job you want isn't the job that you need right now, and sometimes the job you need isn't the one you'd expect. Be aware of opportunities, even unexpected ones—but don't jump at every one that appears to fulfill your dreams. If you're serious about what you're doing, the world will open up to meet you.

Chorus

As a team, you need to be looking out for one another's best interests. Pay attention to what each team member needs in the way of encouragement and improvement; one team member may be a stronger public speaker while another is a stronger researcher. Observe one another's strengths and see what you can learn from them.

Solo

Figure out your own signature sound. It's a complex process that involves much more than listening, even for musicians. Your signature sound is everything about you in a career setting: your appearance, demeanor, work habits, presentation style, and more. Determine where your strengths lie, and play to those strengths while improving on your weaknesses.

Band on the Run

everyone's got a role to play on your team, and not everyone gets the spotlight. you need to avoid the problem of too many lead singers.

t's rare to find lifelong friends working together, whether in business or in a band. The qualities that make a good friend aren't necessarily the same as those that make a good business associate. In this chapter, I break down the story behind forming the core of 38 Special and show how those principles apply to building your own "band," whether for sales, marketing, or operations.

About three months before I graduated from Georgia Tech, I got a call from one of my Jacksonville buddies. He and some other guys I knew had decided to make a serious go at putting a band together. I told them I'd think about it, but when I went back home to Jacksonville, I didn't have to think too hard. It was 1974, and we were all facing a pretty uncertain future. There was nothing else to do in that economic climate, so why not give it a try? What could be better than being in a band for a couple of years while I figured out what to do with my life?

The band had been around for about a month before I graduated, and it was made up of guys I'd known most of my life. I had played with Donnie and our bass player, Ken Lyons, in Sweet Rooster. Don Barnes, our other guitarist, lived up the street from me. I'd also known one of our drummers, Steve Brookins, from the old days. The only one I wasn't familiar with was our other drummer, Jack Grondin, but if the other guys vouched for him, that was good enough for me. It's not typical to have two drummers in a band, of course—the Allman Brothers Band was one of the few groups that did—but for us, it was more a happy accident than a planned musical strategy. We liked both guys too much to decide on just one of them. They had different strengths, and eventually we rotated back and forth when recording an album depending on the style we needed. But from the start, they played onstage in unison, and the noise and power they generated was something to behold.

We'd all been through many bands in the early days, and these guys knew that they had what it took to at least take a shot at making a go of rock music.

They were the sole survivors of that Jacksonville music scene. Where everyone else had gone on to jobs and families and the "real world," they were dedicated to music above all, and that sounded pretty attractive to me.

I was plunging back into rich musical territory. The musical talent in Jacksonville in the late 1960s and early 1970s was easily the equal of any other music scene in the country: Athens, Georgia; Austin, Texas; Seattle; you name it. Jacksonville deserves to be mentioned in the same sentence. I don't know what made the city such a fertile place for Southern rock to develop, except that we were all there together, all feeding off one another, learning from one another, inspiring and pushing one another. We had grown up hearing the same stories about the Old South from our elders, we'd seen the British Invasion, and those influences were combining in every musician's mind to forge a fresh style of music.

When I was in high school, a band called Second Coming was getting a lot of local notice, and for good

> "Unless it's your band, your team, you can't come into a situation thinking you're more valuable than anybody else. If you get your song, your arrangement, your idea played, that's great, but it's still not 'your' band. You've got to be able to go with the flow, to bend a little bit to be a good team member."
> —CARMINE APPICE, DRUMMER FOR OZZY OSBOURNE AND ROD STEWART

reason. Second Coming was one of the first groups that Dickey Betts and Berry Oakley (later essential members of the Allman Brothers Band) played in. We wanted to watch them play, but we were too young to get into the clubs where they were booked, so we had to persuade the kitchen staff to let us listen from the kitchen. We'd have washed dishes if they asked us to. We were that into the music scene.

We'd seen the Allman Brothers, and later Lynyrd Skynyrd, form and go on to huge success. When you see guys you grew up with opening up for The Who, that's a pretty powerful motivator to get your own act together. It wasn't a matter of jealousy; we couldn't be jealous of these guys. They were so talented we just knew that they'd end up making something of themselves. It was more of an inspiration, proof that: *Yes, this CAN be done. It's not just a crazy dream.*

The Band Comes Together

In creating our own band, we were fortunate that almost all of us had known each other for years. We'd played together as kids, hung around together in school, jammed in bands together as teenagers. When you have your own team, you may not be as fortunate to have people with whom you're so familiar. Putting together a team, whether it's for a one-off client engagement, a long-term project, or an indefinite term, requires you to think like a rock star. (No, we don't mean you need to turn your amps to 11 and smash your laptops.) You need to think about the ways your team will mesh together and how the makeup of your team will contribute to your success. Every group has certain defined roles that need to be filled. While you may have two guitarists or two drummers, you still need, at a minimum, one of each. Think of it this way:

"You need to understand what your role is in the team. Jeff was part of a band. I was an employee of Billy Joel. There's a big difference. Billy was my boss, and it was my job to do what he needed me to do. If you're in a job that you don't care for and you didn't set down what you were expected to do right from the start, don't go crying about it later on."
—LIBERTY DEVITTO, CAMP JAM MASTER CLASS DRUMMER AND THIRTY-YEAR VETERAN OF BILLY JOEL'S BAND

- *You need a lead singer.* Every great band has a front man or front woman who's the visible face of the band. This public face is almost always the lead singer, since he or she is the "voice" of the band. You need someone on your team who's dynamic, charismatic, at ease in public, and able to "sing" to the people in the back of the room as well as the front row. Lead singers can be temperamental and egotistical, but there's a reason for that: they're generally the most outsized personalities in a band, and if you've got a good one, you're a leg up on the competition.

• *You only need ONE lead singer.* Actually you can have more than one lead singer (we did in 38), but you need only one lead singer *personality.* Whether or not the lead singer is actually the leader of the band—and in our case, our first lead singer was only one of our driving forces—what's important is that you present a consistent face of your team to the world. In addition, having only one lead singer personality helps cut down on the intra-band battles that will always crop up.

• *You need a counterpoint.* As important as the lead singer is, he needs someone to keep him in check. Think of Mick Jagger and Keith Richards or Bono and The Edge. One of the two is the more flamboyant type, while the other tends to shun the spotlight but has a powerful behind-the-scenes role. If your team is going to succeed, you need to work as an equal team, not in service to your "lead singer." Having someone who commands the respect of both the lead singer and the band preserves the balance, keeping the team from tipping too far in one direction or the other.

• *You need songwriters/creative minds.* Sure, being in a cover band is fun, but you're just walking in someone else's footsteps. If you want to become a real band, you start writing your own songs. Similarly, your team needs creative minds driving your direction, taking your team past what has been tried before. You don't want to be a me-too team, a business equivalent of a cover band; you want to break new ground. Finding creative talent that can develop new ideas and inspire others to do the same is an absolute must.

- *You need a rhythm section.* These are the worker bees of the band, the bass guitarist and drummer. (There are, of course, plenty of bandleaders who play these instruments. Geddy Lee, bass player and leader of Rush, and Don Henley, drummer and coleader of the Eagles, are two well-known examples.) These are the competent professionals, the men and women who reliably and effectively deliver the musical goods. I don't think I need to tell you how essential your "rhythm section" is. There's a good reason that quality rhythm sections are always in demand; a drummer and bass player who can keep time and keep a groove moving with a minimum of fuss are worth their weight in gold records.

- *You need a utility player.* Some musicians can play more than one instrument or can both play an instrument and sing. These double-threats are invaluable in a band, since they can pick up the slack in the studio and on the road if another player falls short. The first time Keith Richards sang lead vocals on a Rolling Stones song happened when an engineer accidentally erased Mick Jagger's vocal track for "You Got the Silver" after Jagger had finished his session and left the country. Similarly, one of our biggest hits came when a guitarist stepped up to the mike on a song that needed a different sound. For your team, this means that everyone needs to have a sense of what everyone else's role is. You need more than one team member with the ability to get up in front of a crowd, you need more than one team member with, say, information technology proficiency.

- *You need collaborators.* Occasionally you'll need to bring in some outside help to finish a job. In our case, we started working with outside songwriters, and they helped inspire us to create some of our best-known hits. Whether your needs are simple, like graphic design for a presentation, or complex, like event planning or delivery logistics, don't hesitate to bring in outside professionals if the work you need done is outside your own skill set. As we'll see many times in this book, doing the same thing over and over doesn't just leave you stuck in the same place; it can send you rolling backward.

"Listen to your fellow musicians and artists. I get a lot more joy out of hearing what they have to say, both musically and on a personal level, than I do telling them about me or trying to impress them in some way. Of course, if they ask, I will engage, but I think when you truly listen, with your ears, with your mind, and with your heart, that's the essence of communication."

—CHUCK LEAVELL, KEYBOARD PLAYER FOR ERIC CLAPTON AND THE ROLLING STONES

Many bands have fallen prey to the all-star myth that if one superstar is amazing, three would be off the charts. That was the thinking in the creation of Cream, rock's first supergroup. Guitarist Eric Clapton had spent the formative years of his career being termed "God" for his instrumental prowess, and bassist Jack Bruce and drummer Ginger Baker were almost equally celebrated. With that much talent, the band couldn't help but put out good music. But it also couldn't help but trip over the egos and attitudes aplenty.

Baker and Bruce in particular feuded with one another, and Clapton would often accuse the two of not listening to anyone but themselves. One show, he proved his point when he stopped playing—and neither of his bandmates even noticed. Cream was an experiment that was almost certainly doomed from the start, as most other "supergroups" have been in the years since then. A three-man band can't have three leaders.

Higher Stakes, Higher Expectations

We weren't superstars, but even so, right off the bat I understood that there were some very different expectations in this new band from any other that I'd been in before. I was living in my parents' house, and I didn't have to work—not because my parents were wealthy, but because they just enjoyed having me back in the house. It was a short-term deal, and the food was good. Why not?

But the other guys in the band weren't quite so fortunate. Some of them married young and had families to support. All had odd jobs; one guy delivered poultry, for instance. They worked all day and rehearsed every night. My hat's still off to them for the effort they put in. These were long days; after a full workday, we rehearsed from 7:00 or 7:30 P.M. until 1:00 A.M. We did this every day, even weekends. That's some serious dedication right there.

I could understand if the guys were a little suspicious of the depth of my commitment. I probably would have been if I were in their shoes. Here they are, putting their entire lives and futures on the line, and they've got this guy in their lineup who's living at home, in effect risking absolutely nothing.

So it was up to me to prove my commitment, to prove that I was a dedicated member of the team and into it every bit as much as the rest of them. I did that, and I convinced them that I was here to stay. It's a good thing for every member of a team to remember: every so often, you need to make sure that everybody on the team knows exactly how dedicated you are, particularly if the members of your team are exposed to different levels of risk.

Contacts are key in any business, and being in a Southern rock band, we had one of the best. In 1974, Lynyrd Skynyrd was in the process of conquering the world. That was the year they released "Sweet Home Alabama," and they'd just come off a nationwide stint opening for The Who. So Donnie Van Zant's big brother, Ronnie, was a perfect contact. We pick up the phone, and Ronnie hooks us up with a record company. Instant fame and fortune, right?

Wrong. Ronnie's reputation was on the line with us, for one thing, so he wasn't going to recommend a terrible group if we weren't at least up to—if not better than—the standards of other groups of the time. More important, though, he wanted us to succeed—and he understood that if we weren't ready, we'd fail without ever getting a chance.

The Band and the Brand

So we practiced, day after day, week after week. We were determined to get 38 Special road ready, and we did it by honing our skills relentlessly. We played every local club we could find in the evenings, banging out covers and the occasional original song. We'd drive anywhere within a fifty-mile radius to get onstage; anywhere we could go and get back in time for work on Monday, we'd be there.

We also got our first lesson in branding when it came to naming ourselves. We'd been practicing for weeks, and even landed live gigs, without even having a name. We had a gig coming up in Gainesville, and the club owner asked us, "What are we supposed to call you guys?"

We thought about it long and hard, day and night. We rehearsed at an abandoned auto parts store in the middle of nowhere, a place we rented for about twenty-five dollars a month. Our name was a constant topic of conversation, in between cranking out songs at ear-splitting volume.

One night the police showed up in force with their sirens blazing, megaphones—the whole bit. They ordered us out into the parking lot, and once we got there, they started making some pretty scary accusations about us disturbing the peace and possibly using some illegal narcotics, among other violations of the law. Things started to get a little heated, and one of the officers said, "You boys better come along peacefully"—and then he lifted his weapon—"or these .38 specials are going to do our talking for us." It was a perfect moment, a perfect name for the band. There was just one problem.

It was a total lie.

Sure, the band rehearsed at the auto parts store. And one time, the cops did come around to see what

was happening. But everything else—the cops showing up (and eventually becoming fans of the band),
the megaphones, the ".38 special" line—was completely
fabricated. It was a story we devised that sounded good
and fit the band's mythology. We told it over and over,
to the point that I almost wished we could carry a little
sheet with the story on it into every radio station we visited. And each time we told it, there was a little part of
me that felt sick inside because we knew it was all completely made up.

The funny thing was, it wasn't the first fake origin
story for the band's name. A&M Records, our record label,
found out that there was once a 1938 Buick Special, so
someone there came up with the story that one of those
Buicks was our first car. That story had the disadvantage
of being both fake and ridiculous, so we dropped it pretty
quickly.

The truth is far more mundane. One of the band's
first fans was an artist who regularly stopped by with
ideas for T-shirts, album covers, and logos. One day he
brought in a simple logo: a circular gunsight with cross-
hairs, and stylized letters that looked like an automotive
font. They spelled out THIRTY EIGHT SPECIAL. It looked cool,
and we had the Gainesville gig coming up, so we went
with it and never looked back. We were building our own
identity at the time, and the idea of being rebellious outlaws seemed an attractive role.

It was part of our agreement that everything we
did was for the greater good. Ironically, it was much
easier getting along with each other then, with all of

us climbing on top of each other, than it was years later when we had success. Why? If I had to pick one word, it would be *jealousy*. I've talked to friends who are successful in all kinds of fields, and they all share a common complaint: the more successful a team gets, the more you start to see jealousy and infighting. There's always competition with people outside the organization, but the further you climb up the ladder, the more competition you see within the organization. Money causes all kinds of problems.

But back in the earliest days of 38, we were filled with creativity and drive, like a whole lot of other young musicians. That's one interesting element of music: a lot of people who are creative—be they artists, painters, musicians, or mathematicians—do their best work when they are young. You can test this theory by looking through your own recordings and notice that your favorite bands did their best work in their twenties, not their forties. Once you start nearing middle age, you're still a great musician—probably, technically speaking, a better one than you are in your twenties. So why does the best work often take place early in a career rather than late?

I think it has a lot to do with what we were experiencing: the positive creative energy that comes from the excitement of a new band and new relationships. Everybody feeds off that, everybody grooves on it, and the competition within the band is healthy—along the lines of, "Here's what I got. Can you top it?" That's the energy that spurs bands to great heights early. John Lennon would write a great song, and then Paul McCartney would try to top it. Can you imagine the genius work that was flying around those sessions?

Going Mobile

We may not have been the Beatles, but we were starting to develop some serious chops of our own. After three to four months of our own sessions, Ronnie came to watch us and proclaimed us ready to hit the road. This was huge, because in those days, without a record to our name, the only way we were going to make any money was by getting out on the road, building a name and a fan base for ourselves one roadhouse bar at a time.

And here's where the idea of sacrifice comes in. Ronnie was going to set us

"I've been playing with Sheryl Crow for ten years. I would say our goal as a band is to make her as comfortable as possible on stage: no distractions from hitting bum notes, no riffing or jamming too far out of context, unless we're all going somewhere and inspired. We try to be consistent, fresh and step it up a notch each night. And have a great time, of course! Beyond that, being a "band" is also about hanging out and being social. . . . Cool and fun to be around. It's like family for us after this long. That's every bit as important as your musical ability. There are a lot of players out there who are as good as you or better. But if you're known to be cool to hang with, you'll most likely get called first."
—GUITARIST PETER STROUD, TEN-YEAR VETERAN OF SHERYL CROW'S BAND

up with an agent who would begin booking us at clubs all over the East. At the time, we'd play a single club for an entire week, from Monday to Saturday, packing up and heading for the next town on Sunday.

Clearly this schedule doesn't fit well with a regular nine-to-five job. If you're going to start going out on the road to make money, you can't really go to your boss and say, "That's it, I'm gone!" if you're only going to be playing one week a month.

It's a big leap, walking away from the known into the unknown—even if the known is driving poultry. We've set out the questions you need to ask yourself before diving into a new venture; those apply here too. But the key with 38 Special at this time was that we were all going through this together. I can't overstate the importance of that fact. You can't overrate confidence. We were the road warriors, the band of brothers—six guys ready to take on the world.

We needed to have that kind of confidence, because the world wasn't quite ready to acknowledge that we existed. We were playing clubs for a week at a time, going from Charleston, South Carolina, to Knoxville, Tennessee, to Lansing, Michigan, for example. We'd make about eight hundred to a thousand dollars—and not each, but *total*. And that money wasn't profit; we had to pay for gas, the hotel, and our vehicle, which always seemed to break down about forty miles from home right at the end of a three-week road trip.

Our first road vehicle was Big Blue, a hand-me-down twelve-foot truck from Lynyrd Skynyrd. We'd pack the gear in Big Blue, and then the rest of us would pile into a Ford Econoline van; we pulled the seats out of the back and threw in mattresses so we could sleep in rotation. It wasn't much, but it was often better than the accommodations we were supposed to stay in.

Back then, bands were on their own to find a place to stay near the club where they were playing. Every once in awhile, a club owner would put us up, but the conditions were dismal. In one city in North Carolina—I can't remember exactly which one; I may have blocked it out—the club owner had a band house. This was the most terrifying, disgusting place you can possibly imagine, with snails crawling out of the drain—that kind of thing. There's a lot of romance and legend attached to the road life, but anybody who thinks that hasn't spent a night in a band house.

Most trips we'd stay at little mom-and-pop hotels. We'd get two rooms, two double beds per room, four guys to a room. Every once in awhile, I'd wake up with a buddy's arm draped over me, but everyone was in the same boat.

We paid ourselves a per diem of $2.50. Yes: $2.50 for everything we needed in a day. Even in the mid-1970s, that didn't get us very far. We'd wake up in the morning, maybe get a banana for breakfast. We'd track down the local all-you-can-eat cafeteria and spend a couple of bucks filling up on some home-style cooking. Then we'd do the gig, and by the time we got back to the hotel room, we'd be starving. So we'd all kick in a quarter and send our driver out to pick up a loaf of bread, a quart of milk, and jars of peanut butter and jelly. We'd stuff ourselves, hit the sack, and in the morning start it all over again.

I was the road manager, which was a bit of a conflict of interest. But we all trusted each other, and it worked out well enough. We'd collect all our earnings, pay out our expenses, and we'd be left with maybe fifteen bucks apiece for three weeks' work. Sometimes we'd get lucky and get a hundred dollars apiece, and sometimes we'd end up drinking all our profits at the club after the gig. You want to talk about paying your dues, we were definitely paying.

Not too long ago, I found some thirty-five-year-old tapes of our earliest performances. And I was surprised in two ways. First, I was surprised at how tight we were for such a young band. We knew what we were doing up there onstage. And second, I was surprised at how lost we were when the songs ended. We'd rip through a song, then there'd be thirty seconds of dead silence while we decided what song to play next. Nobody gave a, "How's everybody doing?" to the audience; nobody acknowledged the need for a stage presence. Musically we were just fine. But we had a ways to go in the whole entertainment-package department.

You don't think about it at the time, but these moments when you're just starting out can be some of the best of your career. Whether you're building products in your garage or working until 3:00 A.M. as a law associate, there's something thrilling about putting so much of yourself into a project. And if you've got a like-minded team around you, so much the better. You're bonding and building connections that you'll remember for the rest of your life.

So the question then becomes: How do you recapture that kind of deep bonding and team building once you've moved on to a higher level? That's a tough one. Chances are you and your employees aren't going to be particularly interested in bunking up with one another, four to a room, once you've gone on and gotten married. And nobody's going to be interested in peanut-butter-and-jelly sandwiches at 2:00 A.M. if you've grown accustomed to eating in restaurants with cloth napkins.

We've found the best way to replicate that kind of bonding is through team-building exercises that force individual team members to rely on one another. You remove them—and perhaps yourself—from their comfort zone and put them into an unfamiliar situation, whether it's ropes courses, or—as in the case of our Camp Jam programs—onstage to rock together. Surviving that kind of stress, physical or emotional, brings you closer and helps you appreciate the strengths of your bandmates in a whole new way. It can be the equivalent of living off quarters, sharing cramped hotel rooms, and journeying from town to town, night after night: you'll build bonds that could potentially last a lifetime.

Verse

When you find a group of like-minded individuals bent on the same goals that you have, hold on to them with both hands. A team in search of a goal is stronger than an individual could ever be.

Chorus

Assess each team member's strengths honestly and openly, and see where each best fits into the overall team. If two people are vying for the top spot, you may need to make a choice, or at the least develop some sort of compromise understanding. But now, when you're building the team, is the time to make sure you start slotting people into their roles.

Solo

Where do you fit into the "band" dynamic? Are you more of a lead singer or a bass player? Think about what it would take to get you to switch "roles." What skill set would you need to improve to get you there?

4

Good Vibrations

keep your eyes on the prize—and on the competition.

Mick Jagger once said that having money is a full-time job. To which I'd add: it's funny how much you can enjoy life when money's not an issue. In the early days of 38, we'd play five sets a night, every single night. That's the way you get really good.

Most rock bands have a similar story in their history, a time when they honed their skills to a razor's edge out on the road. When you're playing that many shows and getting that close to your bandmates, it's literally like a marriage with five or six people involved. You're closer to these guys than you are to your own family.

Every band that broke worldwide started out this same way, from The Who to U2 to Bruce Springsteen and the E Street Band. They'd play clubs night after night, week after week. They'd do whatever they could to stay up, to get in front of one more crowd. They'd sleep on the floor, and if there wasn't a floor somewhere, they'd sleep in a stairwell. And as a result of their early bonding experiences together, they jelled into the cohesive units that made them some of history's greatest bands.

The life of the traveling rocker may be a young person's game, but the truth is, the same rules apply whenever you're starting a new venture, whether it's a new career or a new line of business. You pour your heart and soul into the project, sacrificing sleep and free time, because you believe in what you're doing. You believe so deeply in it that you can't imagine doing anything else. And one day, all those late nights, all those pizza and takeout–Chinese dinners, all those times spent dreaming big start to pay off.

But you don't get to the top of the heap without passing plenty of people along the way. And that's where the idea of competition comes in.

The Battle of the Bands

After a few months on the road, we were locked into a groove. We knew what we were doing onstage. We knew how to read the crowd, how to get them to respond to us, how to get them to pay more attention to us than their beers or their dates. We'd gotten very, very good at our jobs.

But we weren't the only ones. At every level of the music business, there's a circuit—a group of venues that dozens of bands come through every year. Sometimes these bands are on the way up, and sometimes they're on the way down, but they've all got something in common: they want your audience. It doesn't matter who you are or what stage of your career you're in, if you're not looking at an audience and determined to make each one of them think that you're their favorite band, you're not doing your job.

As we made our way throughout the Southeast, with occasional detours to clubs in the Northeast and Midwest, we started to gain something of a reputation. We'd start to see the same faces showing up—or, as we laughed, the same girlfriends—when we rolled into town. We'd started to gain a reputation in certain towns as a must-see band.

Sometimes we arrived at that reputation by accident. I remember one week we spent in Charlotte, North Carolina, playing the Lizard Creek Ballroom, the hottest club in town then. This particular week, we decided to splurge and go to McDonald's for a lunch. Steve Brookins, our drummer, and I were in line when we heard some guys talking in front of us.

"You going to Lizard Creek tonight?" one asked the other. Hearing the name of our venue, our ears perked up. Steve and I glanced at each other.

"No," the other guy responded.

"Aw, man, you've got to go! Everybody's going to be there! The place is going to be packed!" At this, Steve and I looked at each other. *This is pretty cool,* we were thinking. *We've got ourselves a rep!*

"What's going on at Lizard Creek?" the second guy asked. And we listened closely, expecting the first guy to talk all about this great band out of Jacksonville. Not quite:

"They're having a 38-cent special on all drinks!"

The place was jam-packed, and even if it wasn't for us, we took it, and we blew that crowd away. (We always joked that the best name for a band would be "Free Beer," and that night, we came close.)

Misunderstandings aside, we were starting to gain some credibility on the circuit. Club owners knew us to be a reliably hard-rocking band; fans knew we could show them a good time there from the stage. And the more you talk to fans, the more you start to hear about other bands: "Have you guys seen Band X? Those guys rock!" Or, not as good, "Band X is the best band we've seen come through here!"

We didn't take these kinds of statements too seriously because we didn't believe for an instant that there was anybody on the circuit better than us. The approach we took on the road served us well: *You couldn't possibly be better than us. We play too hard; we're too focused on what we want; we're too good at what we do. Eventually we're going to beat you.* A little bit of attitude, properly applied, can go a long way.

Sizing Up the Competition

Here's the thing with attitude, though: if it's the only weapon in your arsenal, you're going to be firing on empty before very long. Attitude backed by talent and drive will take you a long way; attitude backed by sloppiness and inattention to detail will get you shown the door in a hurry.

So how do you keep the attitude? By knowing exactly what the competition is capable of and then figuring out how to one-up them. And you do that by keeping your eye on the competition all the time, even when you'd rather relax and think about anything but work.

When you come offstage and finish a set—or, in the case of business, when you finish a project, a client engagement, a deliverable, or something else with a definite ending point—there's the temptation to relax, kick back, and pat yourself on the back for a job well done. Hey, you worked hard, right? You earned a break.

Sure you did. And sure, you can take a break. But is your competition relaxing? The moment that you complete your task, when you're at the peak of your awareness and connection to your work, that's the precise moment you need to take a look at the competition and see how you stack up.

Here's a more specific example. Back in those days, we'd often play clubs where we were the "name" band in the house from Monday to Thursday, and then on Friday and Saturday we'd open up for a more "well-known" band. Some of these "well-known" groups faded into obscurity within just a few years, and others managed to stick around and make something of themselves, just as we were trying to do. We once opened for REO Speedwagon at the Silver Dollar Saloon in Lansing, Michigan; they'd had a record or two out but hadn't yet broken big nationally. Clearly, though, since they, and other bands like them, were a few steps ahead of us, we could learn something from them.

In a lot of instances, the headliners treat their opening acts as necessary evils. The headlining band doesn't want to get shown up by its opening act, so the opener gets a sliver of stage to perform on, spotlights only a tiny bit brighter than a flashlight, and a weak sound system. (Incidentally, we never handicapped our openers that way. We gave them respect and room because we wanted them to bring their best game. And they respected that. Years after his band opened for us, Huey Lewis called us "real men" for the way we offered them a fair shake.)

The headliner-opener dynamic is an unfair relationship, but it's also a necessary part of paying your dues as a musician. And if you keep your eyes open, you can learn a lot about how to advance in your career. Maybe it's something as simple as the division of labor in getting equipment on and off the stage. (Be your own roadie for a while. Load your own equipment into the van, so to speak. It changes your entire perspective on the world.)

Maybe you could learn something that would be useful on a day-to-day basis, like which clubs took care of you and which ones forced you to take care of them. (When you can't tell whether the restroom or the kitchen is cleaner, it's best to eat somewhere else before the show.)

And maybe you could learn more complex, long-term lessons, like how to divide songwriting royalties or how to go about hiring the right manager or attorney. The people who are only one or two steps ahead of you are often outstanding resources because they've figured out how to make that next move upward.

You can learn something from everyone who's even slightly in competition with you. I've seen musicians and bands make many mistakes, commercial and financial, that they could have easily avoided if they had taken the time to pay attention to what other people were doing around them. Sure, it's nice to take your newly found riches and buy that Mustang you've had your eye on since you were a kid, but maybe that's not quite the smartest long-term investment. And maybe it makes you feel like a big shot to act like a prima donna and order around the rest of your band, but maybe that's not the best way to foster workplace productivity.

So keep your eyes wide open at all times. You'll always learn something new from the competition.

The Next Rung Up the Ladder

Those days on the road were like a second trip through college for me. We were learning so much, but we were also having a hell of a good time, just like in college. The road is a great teacher, and we were receiving an unbelievable education, even if we didn't really pick up on it at the time. We were twenty-two years old, we were independent, and we were driving all over the country: it was the very best of times. All we worried about were our fans and a peanut butter sandwich.

We didn't know it, but sequestering yourself away from the real world and living for nothing but your music makes you become a very, very good band. We were a tightly knit group. We were understanding what we needed to do to get along with five other guys day in and day out, and we were learning how to play to each other's strengths and help each other through weaknesses.

And somewhere along the way, we realized it wasn't just talk; we'd become a very good band. We were starting to develop a following. The crowds were getting larger at every stop, and we'd see familiar faces showing up time and again for our shows. That's pretty heady stuff when you still haven't even recorded a single album. We were playing mostly covers with a few originals salted in, and in the early days of those tours, people weren't coming to see us; they were coming for the beer and some background music. But once you see people coming back, you know you're doing something right.

"When you're onstage, you're five or six guys working together. You've got one mission, and that's what you should be focused on. Your audience doesn't want to see some attitude between the bass player and the drummer; they can pick up on that immediately. It's the same thing in business; if you're not a solid team across the board, your client is going to see it right off the bat."

—LIBERTY DEVITTO, CAMP JAM MASTER CLASS DRUMMER AND THIRTY-YEAR VETERAN OF BILLY JOEL'S BAND

That's a powerful rush: knowing that you're doing something well enough to get people to pay for it more than once. Getting people in the door is the bar's job; making them stay there long enough for the bar to profit off them is your job as a band. And if they like you well enough to start bringing their friends, you'll start finding the club owners are a whole lot friendlier when you're around.

The first impression is absolutely essential, and that's just as true in rock music as it is in business or relationships. Say somebody comes in expecting to hear some familiar tunes and there's a guitarist doing a twenty-minute free-form jazz odyssey. It's not a mystery why that person's turning right around and heading out the door, money still in the wallet instead of the club's register.

We didn't do a whole lot of worrying about our image (we were a bunch of long-haired guys from Jacksonville), but that doesn't mean we weren't aware of it. We didn't show up onstage in costumes, and we didn't try to pretend we were anything other than a group of guys not so different from people in our audiences. We may have acted like "wild-eyed southern boys," as we titled our fourth album, but we weren't quite as reckless as we looked.

When we put all these elements together—the Southern rock lineage, the regular-guy look, the take-on-the-world attitude, the confident musicianship—we were a tight package, and we thought we were ready to take that next step forward. At some point, you start asking yourself, "How much longer do I have to do what I'm doing right now? When does that next door open? And if it's not opening for me, how do I open it myself?"

You've gotten yourself noticed by the crowd in jeans and skirts. Now it's time to figure out how to draw the attention of the people wearing suits.

A Hand Up

There's a famous story about an audition that the Beatles had for Decca Records in London when they were seeking a record deal. Brian Epstein, the Beatles' manager, had the band perform a collection of covers and Lennon/McCartney originals, including "Money (That's What I Want)" and "Memphis, Tennessee," for a group of Decca executives.

Decca *rejected* the Beatles.

That's right. In one of the most colossal mistakes in music history, Decca executives told Epstein that "guitar groups are on the way out," and they passed on signing the Beatles. That should give you an idea of how tough it is to determine whether a band is ready for the big time and how subjective any one executive's opinion really is.

I've always wondered what it is that makes someone in a position of power sit up and take notice. What was it that someone saw in the Beatles or the Rolling Stones or U2? When Jimi Hendrix was tearing up the stage at the Café Wha? in Greenwich Village, what was it that bassist Chas Chandler saw in him to take the first steps toward forming the Jimi Hendrix Experience?

Every band, every business, takes a different route to success, but all have something in common: a network that includes mentors in higher places looking out for them. Sometimes these mentors come along later in the process and sometimes they're around from the start, but no matter what, they're essential to your advancement.

For us, we were fortunate to have a connection to the reigning Southern rock champions of the time, Lynyrd Skynyrd. Had our singer Donnie Van Zant not been the younger brother of Skynyrd's Ronnie Van Zant, our history might have been extremely different—if we'd had a history at all.

While we were out honing our skills at roadside bars and clubs, Skynyrd was becoming one of the biggest bands in the country, taking Southern rock to the farthest corners of the United States and the highest rungs of the charts. They were unbelievably huge, and they were in a position to help us now that we'd shown we were worthy.

Once we convinced Ronnie that we were serious about making a go of a musical career and were ready to go into the studio, he began pulling some strings with the help of Skynyrd's manager, Peter Rudge. Rudge was a legend in the music business; he'd managed tours for the Rolling Stones, The Who, and Golden Earring, among many other bands, and he knew how to get things done. Ronnie told Peter that he needed to check out "my little brother's band."

We knew things were starting to happen, but we didn't stop touring waiting around for something to break loose. We were still living off our $2.50 a day, still beating the bushes and building a base one fan at a time.

Rudge helped set up auditions for the major labels; Arista and Clive Davis came to see us, as did CBS, but they passed on us. Fortunately, A&M Records didn't. Back then, A&M was known as the last of the big independent record labels; it was not part of any big conglomerate. That independence, that willingness to look at more than the bottom line, was a rare commodity even in those days, and one you can't find at all today. And it was an approach that would end up saving our career a few years down the line.

What drew A&M to us? Was it our talent, our showmanship, our potential? Probably some combination of all of those. But we were also playing one of the hottest styles of music in the country at that moment, Southern rock, and we were playing it as well as anybody who wasn't already signed to a label.

Southern rock blends the folk music of the Appalachians with the blues of the Mississippi Delta, and then it slathers these two classic forms of American music with an aggressive attitude and a restless spirit. More than most other forms of music, Southern rock relies heavily on storytelling in its lyrics. The world that Southern rock bands sang about was an almost mystical place of swamps, gators, whiskey, and women who had done you wrong. It was as colorful a place as any novel ever described, and the musicians playing Southern rock thought of themselves as gunslingers bent on conquering the nation. It's no wonder so many people responded to it so quickly.

By the mid-1970s, Skynyrd, the Allman Brothers, the Charlie Daniels Band, the Marshall Tucker Band, the Outlaws, and others were all taking the country by storm. And I have to be honest: I think A&M wanted a Southern rock band of its own—a trophy, if you will. I'd like to think they saw something special in us, but looking back and being objective, I sure don't see anything that was special about us back then. We weren't doing anything that the larger bands weren't doing better than us.

But sometimes all you need is an opening. All you need is the right partner. Would we have made the same splash if we'd managed to draw the attention of one of the huge conglomerates? Maybe. Maybe not. We'd have gotten a huge push out of the gate, but we wouldn't be permitted any missteps. And trust me, your mentor, your senior partner, is going to need to be understanding; the chances are slim indeed that you'll be flawless right from the start.

So now you've got the opportunity to put your product in front of the entire country. How do you handle it? Here's one tip that we learned from our first large-scale gig: hang together but don't cling together.

Thrown in the Deep End

In the mid-1970s, we may have been a green Southern rock band, but we were now sharing a record label with one of the most popular musicians of the time. Peter Frampton had released *Frampton Comes Alive!* on A&M Records, and was touring the country to vast acclaim. A&M decided to throw us in the deep end of the pool by having us open for Peter Frampton before we'd even recorded our first record.

It was beyond generous. Frampton didn't need any kind of support act; he was selling out every arena he visited. In fact, I'm not even sure we got paid anything for that tour beyond our expenses. But we were an unknown band without even a record to our name taking the stage with a superstar. No pressure, right?

We opened the tour at the West Palm Beach Coliseum and were as nervous as we could be. The previous week, we'd been playing clubs in front of a couple of hundred people, and here we were about to go out on a forty-foot stage in front of ten thousand people.

We did it. We got out there and played our hearts out, and I don't remember a thing. The crowd cheered us, so we must have done well. But it was there and it was gone, a half-hour passing by before we even knew what happened.

Still feeling the rush of the crowd, we started asking around. "How did we do? How did we do?" And everyone had the same answer:

"Guys . . . you need to spread out more."

We were on an enormous stage, but we were six guys used to crowding around one another in clubs. So there we were: six guys huddling together in the middle of a huge stage. It was another learning experience for us: if you've got the stage available to you, use every inch of it. Bonding together as a team is important, sure, but not while you're onstage.

That's a small example of how naive we were, and it speaks to a larger point: you'll make mistakes, but be sure to make each one only once. Every night after the show, we'd talk about what worked and what didn't. Sometimes the mistakes we made were so small that nobody outside the band would notice, but we needed to make sure we caught everything. Keeping eye contact during tricky sections, keeping our ears open to hear how our bandmates are progressing through the song: these are the kinds of small but important elements of performance that we needed to master in order to be a top-tier rock band.

In the same way, you need to understand exactly what makes your team function at its highest level. Are you a deadline-driven bunch, or can you function independently? Are you keeping in close enough communication that you're working at the highest levels of efficiency? As your team learns to work together, you'll learn where the rough spots lie, and you can take steps to correct these problems before the rest of the world catches sight of them.

Verse

No matter how much you want success, someone out there is willing to work harder than you. The question is, are they willing to work smarter? Make sure you use your mind as well as your effort in order to achieve your goals as quickly as possible.

Chorus

Get in the trenches. Work together, and hang together. Function as a team as often as possible. You don't need to get an apartment together or live four to a hotel room on the road. But if you as a team can get comfortable with one another, you can function that much more effectively.

Solo

Look at your company through the eyes of a competitor. What weaknesses do you see that you, as a "competitor," could exploit? What advantages does a competitor have over your company? By adjusting your perspective, you can get an idea of where your own soft spots lie.

No Direction Home

THERE ARE TIMES THAT YOU'LL WONDER WHY YOU'RE DOING WHAT YOU'RE DOING, TIMES WHEN YOU WONDER IF YOU SHOULD JUST GIVE IT ALL UP AND TAKE A SAFER ROUTE.

Musicians never forget the first time they hear their own song on the radio—or, in my case, the first time they *almost* hear their song on the radio.

We'd recorded our first album, the album we'd waited our entire lives to make, and we were in Jacksonville at the local radio station, where the DJ was throwing us a little hometown love. He'd invited us into the studio and told us to bring along a copy of our record. At long last, we were going to be on the radio! We told everyone we knew, and everyone we could get in contact with was listening that day.

Our first mistake was to bring the entire band into the studio. The DJ would ask us something simple, like, "How long have you guys been together?" and there would be a solid blast of six voices: "Blahblahblah . . ." Nobody could hear anything. The lesson: send one or two people to do the press.

Then the DJ asked for the record. We handed it over, and he set it on the turntable. "Here's the moment you guys have been waiting for," he said. "Ladies and gentlemen, the first song by a brand-new band, 38 Special." He dropped the needle, the song started, and—EEEEEERRRRRRRRRR!!!

The needle skidded all the way to the center. "Wow, sorry about that," the DJ said. "Let's give that another try."

EEEEEERRRRRRRRRR!!!

It was a faulty disc. Our big break, our chance to get on the radio, and we'd brought a bad record. That took a while to live down, especially because we couldn't get enough interest from even the local radio stations to get another song from either of the first two albums played on the radio.

When we finally did start hearing our music on the radio regularly, it was perfect. For a moment, you're thinking, "I'm on the radio. I am *on the radio.*"

Peter Rudge, Lynyrd Skynyrd's manager, decided to take us on as another of his bands, and after we came off the

Money (That's What I Want)

Frampton tour, he sat us down and gave us the next chapter of our education: how money ought to work for us. We were all sitting in his office as Peter looked us over.

"How have you guys been paying yourselves?" he asked.

We looked at each other. *Paying* ourselves? It had never been much of an issue. We never had enough money to really "pay" ourselves beyond a few bucks at a time. By the time we got off any stand of club dates, we usually had to pay to get repair work done on the truck or cover other expenses. Sometimes we even had to go into debt to our parents to make ends meet, and we had to pay them off as well.

Peter nodded, understanding the trials of a young band. "Did you pay yourselves a per diem?"

We nodded. We did do that.

"How much?"

"Two dollars and fifty cents."

"No, no," he said, smiling at what must have been our misunderstanding of the question. "How much did you pay yourselves each day to eat and live off of?"

"Two dollars and fifty cents," we repeated, proud of ourselves and utterly unaware of how absurdly small a sum it was even in the mid-1970s. We told the story of the quarter contributions for peanut butter sandwiches and quarts of milk, and Peter and his associates shook their heads in disbelief.

"Well, how much are you paying yourselves in salary?"

It wasn't an issue. We had never even thought of the idea of paying ourselves a salary. But that was about to change.

"Here's what we're going to do," Peter said. "Each of you guys will get a hundred dollars a week in salary. Every week, whether or not you're on the road. And when you're on tour, you'll get a per diem of ten dollars a day."

All of a sudden, the money we were earning from playing local clubs was going into a corporate structure, not just straight back out the door. We couldn't believe it. A salary! And ten bucks a day for food? We were *rich!*

That, I recall, was the first time we reached a significant financial benchmark. All of a sudden we realized we would have some money at the end of the day. We might actually be able to put a few dollars away for a rainy day. Heck, we could each have our *own* quart of milk and loaf of bread if we wanted!

It was a pleasant lesson to learn, but one that took our attention: money is too important to be left as an afterthought. You should be thinking about the financial aspect of your career long before you get paid, not when you've got the cash in your hand, metaphorically or literally, ready to spend.

In short, when it comes to money, get help. Bring in somebody who knows how to work money better than you do. If you're already a financial mastermind, congratulations. But it's always an extremely good idea to bring in somebody to serve as an extra and impartial pair of eyes.

And while you're at it, make sure to get your own attorney. Early in our career, we made the mistake of staying in our manager's stable for everything we needed: accountant, attorney, everything. When we had some minor disagreements later on (and they really were just that, minor), we suddenly found that the attorneys and accountants we'd been relying on weren't necessarily looking after our interests first and foremost.

We were extremely lucky that we weren't fleeced by an unscrupulous manager. We were so naive back then, and I can see how musicians can get taken in and lose almost everything. Everyone from Sting to Billy Joel has lost millions to shady managers and accountants. We had some minor disagreements over publishing rights to certain songs early in our career, but those songs are all but worthless from a financial perspective. If nobody wanted to put them on the radio back then, they certainly aren't going to want to now.

We didn't know it at the time, but we were building a support team to go with the team that we already had in place. But while we knew what to look for in, say, a drummer or a bass player, we didn't quite know what questions to ask an attorney or an accountant. We didn't know to follow a few ironclad rules for building a support structure:

• *A friend of a friend is good only to a point.* There's a reason family members shouldn't go into business with one another. The hard decisions that business demands often run against the grain of family relationships. Similarly, if you're looking to bring on a new member of your team, make sure you're doing it because this is the best person to handle the job, not because the person happens to be an in-law of someone on your team. That's not to say that relations and acquaintances can't handle a business relationship, just that those kinds of connections shouldn't be a qualification in and of themselves.

• *Bring the specialists on board, not the generalists.* If you're going to require a contract attorney, find yourself a contract attorney. If you need an accountant to handle your small-business cash flow, don't hire an accountant who specializes in individual tax return preparation. It seems obvious (you wouldn't hire a dentist to perform your annual physical, would you?), but all too often, we want to take the path of least resistance, trusting that someone with roughly the correct graduate degree will instantly understand the intricacies of our particular situation.

• *Find people who can show you, not just tell you, that they're looking out for your interests.* It's easy to find someone who wants a piece of your action, particularly after you've had some success. What's not so easy is finding someone who's willing to stake his or her success on your own—in other words, to demonstrate commitment to you in hard dollars-and-cents terms. Once we made the break from our manager's accountant, we took on an accounting firm that agreed to work with us in return for a percentage of our revenue. Although it wasn't a significant paycheck early on, their fortunes were tied to our own. And they agreed that once we achieved a certain level of success, one where their percentage would net them fees far beyond what was customary, they would return to a more standard financial relationship. Those are the kinds of partners you want.

• *Find people you can grow with—scalable partnerships, so to speak.* A one-person operation might gain you a new friend and ally, but will that one person be able to handle the workload if you break large? And if you go with a larger firm, will it have the resources to dedicate to you as your own career grows—as we all know it will? Think about what your new "teammates" can do for you not just now, but a year from now and five years from now.

So with our new team in place, we set about making records. We did what we knew best: straight-ahead Southern rock 'n' roll, heavy on the blues, guitar, and attitude. The problem was that just about every other Southern rock band out there was doing the exact same thing. We released a self-titled CD, often standard for a first album, but a move that didn't do much to set us apart from the pack. We sounded a whole lot like everyone else, and people picked up on that—even if they didn't pick up the album.

What everyone did seize on was the connection between 38 Special and Lynyrd Skynyrd. Just about every review mentioned the Van Zant family bond, most running like this one, from the August 11, 1977, issue of *Rolling Stone:* "38 Special is the second rock band in the

Van Zant family, but any similarity between Donnie Van Zant's group and his older brother's Sturm und Drang aggregation, Lynyrd Skynyrd, is purely genetic."

And it got worse: "The instrumentation is the standard combo of Stones chord patterns and Claptonesque leads, but the overall playing is much less frenetic than you might expect—part of the arrangement in a very calculated sense."

The reviewer was more on target than even he knew. We were indeed just a reflection of our influences at that point. We weren't bringing anything new to the table. We weren't offering listeners anything they couldn't get better somewhere else.

Plenty of Southern rock bands had already carved out space on the radios of America in the late 1970s. Why did we think we could break through by just imitating what they'd done? That's a key point to remember, whether you're selling rock 'n' roll or rocking chairs. Why imitate what someone else is doing? Chances are, you won't do it as well as they do. And if someone's looking for that particular product, why would they choose the imitation over the original?

38 Special sold only about twenty-five thousand copies. We continued touring around the country, but we weren't connecting with an audience. We knew things should be going better than they were, and so we knew we had to get back into the studio and record our next album. We assumed that we'd just had a rough start and that we'd get the ship righted with album number 2. But before we could get started on recording, we suffered the worst kind of tragedy.

The Greatest Loss

On October 20, 1977, we were in the studio rehearsing. We were a couple of weeks away from going into the studio and feeling that kind of nervous energy that comes from loving what you do but knowing you have to do it better. We didn't know it, but our perspective, on both life and music, was about to change forever.

Our tour manager, Dennis Thomas, walked into the studio, and he had the kind of look on his face that you never want to see because you know something horrible has happened.

"Hey, guys," he said quietly, "Skynyrd's plane went down."

Silence. We couldn't believe it. Skynyrd were our big brothers—literally in Donnie's case, and figuratively for the rest of us. We'd grown up with these guys, and they'd taken us under their wing. That day, we left the studio lost in our own thoughts.

By the time I got home, the phone had started ringing. We were trying to get any kind of information we could. We later found out that some of our friends had survived, including Billy Powell, who'd been a Cub Scout friend of mine. But it was later confirmed that Ronnie Van Zant and many others aboard that plane did not.

We were devastated. We'd lost family in every sense of the word. These guys were our musical inspiration, but even more than that, they were our friends. We couldn't even imagine a world without Lynyrd Skynyrd in it.

But even in our grief, we knew we had to go on. It wasn't just that Ronnie would have wanted us to do that. We had a bond among ourselves, an obligation to the band, to our families, to the music. We had to keep going. There was never a question.

One of my most favorite moments as a musician came while playing with Ronnie, and at a completely unexpected moment. We owned a rehearsal space in Jacksonville next door to where Skynyrd had set up its own recording studio. We regularly hung out there and lay down tracks, sometimes as a band, sometimes in various combinations of the Jacksonville musical crew.

One night after the session was over, Ronnie asked me to hang around. He had a new song he wanted me to work on. Called "Four Walls of Raiford," it was the story of a man on the run, a Vietnam veteran who'd been caught stealing to feed his family. The man was leaving behind a wife and two kids, and he knew the government he'd fought for was going to shoot him down. It was a desperate, painful song in the tradition of the finest blues of the twentieth century.

Ronnie sang the tune for me (he never wrote anything down, always kept it all in his head), and we started to work out a classic folk arrangement. It was past one in the morning, but we sat down in two chairs, face to face, and nailed that song in just a few takes. It was just Ronnie singing and me playing the dobro, a very resonant guitar— and it's one of my favorite tracks I've ever worked on.

Ronnie died before the song came out on an album. But in 1987, while compiling an album of outtakes and B-sides, some of Skynyrd's producers uncovered

"Four Walls." They added a lot of instrumentation—keyboards, guitars, bass, echo on Ronnie's voice—that to me killed the haunting, lonesome feel of the original.

Years later, I was on the road and someone came up to me and thanked me for that song. I nodded in appreciation and said, "I wish you could have heard the original, before they added all the instruments."

What the fan said next absolutely floored me. "That's the one I'm talking about! They released it!" It turns out that the original demo was on a new box set. I went out and bought that set the next day, and hearing it again in its original form brought that night back to me as if it had just happened. I was thrilled and sad all at once, but I'm so glad that the original version is now out there and available.

Back Down to the Ground

So it was with heavy hearts that we went back into the studio to record *Special Delivery*, our second album. And we couldn't believe it at the time, but we certainly can now: it sold even worse than our first album. And with Peter Rudge and other management we shared with Skynyrd occupied with lawsuits and other issues relating to the crash, we decided we had to move on.

I've never had a lower point professionally than I did then. We were still grieving from the loss of our friends, and now our first two albums had sold fewer than fifty thousand copies combined. These days, that would be instant career death. (Today you get dropped from your record label if you sell 3 million copies of your first CD but "only" 1 million of your second.)

With our manager distracted and our record sales scraping rock bottom, we fell apart. We told the record company that we were at home working on new songs for the third album. But the truth was, we weren't touring, and we weren't playing anywhere. The money had run out, so that hundred dollars a week we'd been enjoying for the last couple years was no more.

We'd gone from being on a rocket straight upward—playing in sold-out arenas in front of tens of thousands of fans, record deals, applause at every turn— to being back at ground level. Worse than ground level. With no more money from the band, many of us had to go on unemployment. We'd wear sunglasses and ball caps to the unemployment line; we were back in our hometown, after all, and we'd left as rock heroes. How bad would it look if we were caught in the unemployment line?

But that wasn't the big issue. The real issue was that if the record company picked up on the fact that we were collecting unemployment, that we had no manager, that we weren't playing gigs or touring at all, we assumed they'd drop us. Then we'd have no hope whatsoever.

I started to think that maybe this was it, that maybe it was time to dust off the old T-square and put my architectural degree to use after all. Sure, we had been all over the road and gotten local coverage, but our songs weren't getting played on the radio because we weren't offering anything new. We were this close to going back to real jobs. You go from having nothing to apparently having everything you've ever wanted, making nothing to making what seemed like a millionaire's wages. And then when you lose it, it's worse than if you'd never had it at all.

So what do you do if you're facing what looks like the end of your dreams? You could give up, certainly. Plenty of bands did just that, never even becoming famous enough to warrant a "Where are they now?"

You could also take an honest look at what got you to where you are. Did popular tastes change, as they do so often in popular music? We were fortunate in that one sense. Tastes hadn't passed us by; we hadn't even caught up to them in the first place. We just weren't delivering the kind of music that could break us out of the pack. We needed something, or someone, to help us take the next step forward.

So we got up all the courage we had and contacted a confidant we had at the record company named Mark Spector, an A&R (artist and repertoire) man who had a reputation for shepherding bands through difficult times. We came clean to him and told him how far we'd fallen. To our immense relief, not only did A&M not drop us, but label cofounder Jerry Moss decided that we'd be receiving some more money to put together some demos for the next record.

"We signed you guys," Mark said, "not Peter Rudge."

So we started preparations for the third record. We didn't say anything to one another about this being our final shot. We didn't need to. Everyone knew exactly how high the stakes were.

Verse

Your career will take a downturn. There's no way around it. So prepare for that downturn by surrounding yourself with the smartest and most effective support team possible. They'll pick you up when you're down and help you find a way out when you're lost.

Chorus

As a team, brainstorm the kinds of assistance that you'll need to function at the highest possible level. Be honest with each other; try to break down where you can foresee problems cropping up. Do you see the possibility of a leadership battle? A lack of effort? A lack of focus? Catch it now and perhaps hurt a couple of feelings, or wait until later when it costs a couple of jobs.

Solo

Start making a list of all the key roles you'll need filled to help your team achieve its goals. Will you need marketing assistance? Legal advice? Accounting and payroll help? Whatever it is, start lining up your support team now.

6

Satisfaction

A LITTLE SUCCESS CAN BE A WONDERFUL THING—BUT DON'T FORGET THAT A LITTLE SUCCESS CAN BE MORE DAMAGING THAN NONE AT ALL.

I magine two young, newly formed bands, both equally talented and both with an equal love of music. Both start out playing cover tunes at parties, entertaining their friends and family with "Louie Louie" and "Twist and Shout." Both see the road wide open before them, and both assume it's going to lead them straight to worldwide success.

Fast-forward ten years. One of those bands is selling out stadiums, and one's still playing "Louie Louie" on Tuesdays at the airport Holiday Inn. What happened along the way to send two bands from the same starting point to two totally different destinations?

Certainly passion helps, as does talent. There's also the matter of will, of drive, of dedication. You need to be able to make a connection with your fans beyond playing on their nostalgia with cover tunes—or, to put it in more business-oriented terms, slapping a "New! Improved!" tag on the face of your product. You need to provide something that's both comfortably familiar and enticingly new at the same time. (It's not easy.)

But every band—every company—has faced in its history a moment of crisis, a point at which a decision irrevocably alters the future.

The Proverbial Switching of Gears

We didn't know it—you never do at the time—but we were about to make the most important decision of our career.

We'd formed back in 1974 at a time when Southern rock was at its peak. The Allman Brothers Band was in full swing; Lynyrd Skynyrd's "Sweet Home Alabama" was all over the radio. We loved these guys, and we did everything we could to sound just like them. And although we didn't realize it at the time, that was a serious problem.

We blended a little Allmans, a little Skynyrd, a little country, and a little rock 'n' roll and came up with something that sounded a little good, but only a little. We didn't have an identifiable sound or direction. I listen to our first album now, and I think it's atrocious. There are some moments on it when you can hear some promise, but when you think of where we were then and where we eventually evolved to—well, good grief, where did that come from?

Simple. We realized that we'd learned a great deal from our inspirations, and it was time to start making our own mark on the world. At some point, you need to understand when your mentors have given you all that you need to get going. You can attend leadership seminars and breakfasts all year long, filling your head with the latest in management theory, sales force motivational tips, and organizational insight. But at some point, you need to step out from under the shadow.

We Need a Hit

There's nothing wrong with being the kind of band that plays a Holiday Inn, just like there's nothing wrong with running a one-person mail-order business out of your basement. But if you've got bigger dreams, you've got to understand what's necessary to achieve them.

In music, what defines success—at least, the kind of success that gets you more record deals—is the hit song. You've got to get played on the radio. These days, of course, there are other ways to create a following, but back then, you needed that hit single.

So how exactly do you get that hit single? That's the million-dollar question. Anybody who has to ask doesn't know, and anybody who knows isn't telling. Certainly nobody was giving us any clues in 1979. We'd made some tentative steps in a new direction on our second album, and it had stiffed even worse than our first. So clearly half-measures weren't going to do it.

We knew we needed a change, and we broke it down this way:

- *We needed to market ourselves differently.* Southern rock wasn't yet a cliché, but it was pretty close. There are only so many songs you can write about gators and whiskey and swamps and shotguns and your woman doing you wrong before you start to become a parody of yourself. We were headed that way, if we weren't there already.
- *We needed to stop following in the footsteps of our forefathers.* Everything we were trying to do had already been done by people who were much, much better at it than we were. What's the point of trying to do something when you're only 50 or 75 percent as good as the best? Why not break out and be the best in your own field?
- *We opened our minds.* We were a bit younger than most of the big Southern rock bands of the day, so we were open to new sounds, new ideas. New Wave was getting big right at this time. Although there aren't two bands around more different than Lynyrd Skynyrd and the Cars, we realized that we could learn new musical techniques from both of them. More important, we realized nobody else was doing that. We took the blinders off and exposed ourselves to a much larger spectrum of music that we could draw inspiration from.

- *We didn't know what we were going to do, but we knew it had to be different.* This was the hardest part of all: not knowing where we'd end up. We didn't know what we were going to come up with, but we knew it had to be different from what we'd done before.

So how do you create something different? You can't go out and consciously try to break new ground. You'll end up with a mess or, worse, something that looks/sounds/feels as if it's trying to be different—and if there's one thing you don't want to do when you're creating something new, it's to get caught trying. There's nothing less funny than someone trying to be funny, and there's nothing more off-putting to consumers than a product trying desperately to bill itself as new when it's not.

In music, you don't just clock in and say, "It's 9:00 A.M. Time to write." Some of the best ideas come at the most unexpected times. For instance, Keith Richards once awoke in the middle of the night in a Florida hotel room with what he thought was a killer guitar riff running through his head. He sang the tune into a portable tape recorder, then fell back asleep. The next morning—amid forty-five minutes of snoring—Keith located those eight notes again and turned them into the Rolling Stones classic "Satisfaction."

The lesson? Keep your mind open and a note pad or PDA handy at all times. Inspiration can hit at uncommon moments.

That's not to say you don't take an active role in the creative process. You consciously open your mind to ideas and influences around you to see what's going on not just in your own corner of the world, but elsewhere as well. For us, that meant listening to more than our favorite stations on the radio, listening to what was going on all over the dial at the time. We knew we had to get away from country rock—both the sound and the lyrical content.

For you, it may be time to look at your product, your niche, your competitive space with fresh eyes. You'll be amazed at what opens up before you when you stop looking at your business from the same perspective. We all live in comfort zones—the equivalent of a predictable, comfortable, verse-chorus-verse song—but every so often, you've got to step out of the confines and *jam.*

We were determined to make a change, and that meant bringing in some new blood to help us put the records together. We started by looking for a new producer. That didn't sit so well with the record company, especially when they began flying in guys who didn't seem to know exactly what to do with us.

Producers are responsible for bringing out the best in a band. But that doesn't necessarily mean they knew

how to deal with people. I recall one guy who told us that
if necessary, he could fly in some "big guns" to help us
out—in other words, he was going to have session musicians play *our* music on *our* album! We told him thanks
but no thanks. We were a little cocky and full of ourselves
back then, but in that case
I think it was the right
thing to do. You can
hire people to help
bring your vision to
life, but at the end
of the day, you
need to live and
die by what you
create yourself.

> "When
> you're a part of a
> team, you need to have a
> common vision. That's the
> problem that most teams face,
> that everyone isn't on the same
> page. You all need to
> understand what you're
> striving for."
> —DON FELDER,
> FORMER GUITARIST, THE
> EAGLES

The solution
ended up being right
under our noses. We'd
known a young studio
guy by the name of Rodney
Mills for quite awhile. He'd been an engineer on a lot of
records we liked, including "Sweet Home Alabama," and
he'd worked with everyone from the Atlanta Rhythm
Section to James Brown, giving each a sound that
popped off the record. The engineer handles the sophis-
ticated technical details of a record's creation, like making
sure the mikes are placed properly and everyone's part is
getting recorded at the proper levels. He's there to exe-
cute the vision of the producer, who's the equivalent of a
director on a movie set. The producer works on a concep-
tual level with the artist, helping to arrange the song and

sift through ideas to find the ones that best fit the overall concept of the song.

We weren't exactly in a position to dictate to the record company that we wanted this unknown kid producing and engineering our record. But we knew we had to get some groove into our records, and we knew from looking at our record collections that Rodney could deliver that kind of groove. So we went to bat for Rodney with the record company, and they agreed to give him a chance.

Now we had a new direction in our music, a new location for making records, and a new producer to help us bring those songs into the light. We had our minds open to all kinds of new influences, but we still had this unshakeable core—a real and credible Southern pedigree. No matter what, we were still going to be influenced by the blues, by country, by the British Invasion bands, by the soul music we all grew up listening to. We didn't know what we were doing; we didn't say, "Why, we're combining country, rock, and pop!" while we were doing it. We'd just put something together and ask each other, "You ever heard anything like this?" If the answer was no, great! We had something to work with!

We also started working with outside writers, as we detail in the next chapter. We can't emphasize enough the value of collaborators in your own business environment.

As we worked on our next album, *Rockin' into the Night,* it all came together in a great victory. After a conscious effort to make a change, we did it, even with the obstacles and the odds stacked against us. We went from selling 25,000 records to selling 250,000 and notching our first Top 40 single.

It wasn't just that the fans picked up on what we were doing, though connecting with more people than we ever had before was certainly the most rewarding thing. Reviewers were also starting to pay attention to us. Critics who had torn us to pieces on our first two albums suddenly started loving us, writing that we were now the best thing to come out of Southern rock. With *Rockin' into the Night,* we became *the* band that emerged from the South carrying the banner of Southern rock and holding it high. I can't fault the writers for changing their minds, because we weren't the same band on our third album that we'd been on the first two. If people thought we were the best band in the South, it's because we'd made ourselves the best.

There's Always a Faster Gun

But as good as we were, we still had much to learn. Here's a cautionary tale about the dangers of thinking too highly of yourself. Imagine you're in our position after *Rockin' into the Night.* You're on the rise. You're feeling good about yourself, your team, your prospects. Doors are opening for you left and right. It's all happening for you now, and it's all going right. Sure, you're on a low level now, but you're on the way up. Right? And as good as you're getting, you know it's only a matter of time before you're on top. After all, there's not anybody out there who can top you, is there?

Guess what. There is. There always is.

In 1979, we had the idea that no matter who you were, we were going to beat you. No matter how hard you thought you played, we'd play harder. No matter how much you rocked the crowd, we'd rock them longer. Part of it was that whole Southern rock competition: we used to do everything we could to beat up on our competition. We loved those guys off the stage, but on it, we were out for blood. Everybody understood that because everybody knew the game.

"We played a concert TV special in Central Park where Sheryl invited some very special guests. At one point, Eric Clapton is walking offstage as Keith Richards is walking on. My head was spinning, having finished 'Little Wing' with Eric and launching into 'Happy' with Keith! A dream come true, to say the very least. Keith is staring me in the face, shouting, 'Go, man, go!' for a solo. . . . And I'm thinking, 'I hope somebody's getting a picture of this!' "
—GUITARIST PETER STROUD, TEN-YEAR VETERAN OF SHERYL CROW'S BAND

We played the game well enough to attract the attention of some larger bands. We were invited to go on tour with ZZ Top, a band we'd always admired. These days, everyone knows ZZ Top for the beards and the Texas attitude. Back then, they'd had huge early success with their brand of Tex-Mex blues rock. Billy Gibbons, their guitarist, was as good as they came, and Dusty Hill and Frank Beard (who, ironically, sported only a mustache) were an all-star rhythm section. But they were coming off a long hiatus. Nobody knew how much they had left; nobody knew whether they were still the best they were at what they did.

We were opening for ZZ Top, and that first show may have been one of our best ever. We killed it out there. The crowd was going crazy, and they brought us back for an encore, something you don't usually see from opening acts. There was a charge in the crowd that night, a charge onstage, and we could all feel it. I remember saying to our drummer Jack, "That little old band from Texas better be on their game tonight!" Sure, we loved and respected ZZ Top, but that didn't mean we didn't want to blow them off the stage.

So after we cooled down, I took up my usual spot over by the corner of the stage. You can learn a tremendous amount by watching your competition in their element, and I believed in watching the best at work to see what I could learn. And boy, did I get an education that day.

I was at a place in the wings of the stage where I could see the entire layout. A three-sided scrim had come down to conceal them from the audience. And then the lights went down. It was that perfect moment, the moment of anticipation, when absolutely anything could happen. ZZ Top's classic voiceover introduction boomed out over the audience, "Ladies and gentlemen, please welcome that little old band from Texas . . ." And then it happened.

The curtains rose. Billy Gibbons and bassist Dusty Hill had grown their soon-to-be-world-famous beards, and the world was getting their first look at ZZ Top's new style. They marched to the edge of the stage in a cool choreographed routine, playing "I Wanna Thank You." It was a slow, slinky groove, and these guys had mastered it. And as I watched them rolling out this whole new vibe, I remember thinking, *Uh-oh. It's over.*

We thought we were pros. But we weren't even playing the same game as these guys—at least not yet. You can achieve a certain level of excellence, a certain level of skill, but no matter what, there's always someone out there doing it better than you. It's a tough lesson to learn, but one you'd better learn very early.

I can't say I consciously thought all this as I watched Billy Gibbons that night onstage in his suit and hat looking like some smooth Baptist preacher. But I could tell that these guys were the epitome of cool. They had the swagger. They were cool without even trying to be cool. They were, as we used to say in those days, *slinging it.*

That night, ZZ Top was doing two things that knocked us down a notch. First, they had that easy, essential cool. You can't fake cool, and you can't force it. You either have it or you don't. And they had that attitude, and it was spilling off the stage.

The other lesson they taught us that night was how to approach playing music. Two different guitarists can play the same notes, the same song, and generate completely different emotions in the listener. ZZ Top figured out how to sling it. They could make their music groove like nobody else, and they connected with the audience in a way we couldn't even imagine yet.

I will never forget that night. Never. It was a tough lesson to learn, but an important one: no matter how good you are, there's always a quicker draw out there.

You've got to make sure you see them before they see you. That's how the best bands survive, and that's what we were aiming to do.

But first, we had to come up with a follow-up to the most successful album of our career. (Nothing like a little pressure, right?)

The first taste of success is wonderful. The thing is, everyone's going to expect an encore, and you'd better be ready to deliver.

Verse

There's nothing quite like success, especially hard-earned success. But to prepare yourself for success, sometimes you have to move off the beaten path. If you're just replicating what someone else has already done, what incentive is there for the customer to pay attention to you rather than the original?

Chorus

Conduct periodic team examinations to review what the team is doing well and what requires improvement. And don't skip over the praise part. Helping people understand what they do well is essential to furthering professional development.

Solo

Spend a week observing the successes of industries
other than your own. Watch how other industries,
from video rentals to coffee shops, handle crises
and capitalize on opportunities. Watch others in
action, and see what you can learn from them.

7

Welcome to the Jungle

BEFORE LONG, YOUR HARMONIOUS TEAM WILL HAVE DISAGREEMENTS. HOW YOU HANDLE THE EARLY ONES WILL MAKE THE DIFFERENCE BETWEEN TRIUMPH AND DISASTER.

t's going to happen, like it or not: the rift. Your team is made up of individuals, and individuals never agree on everything. In a band, you hope there will be no major disagreements, the kind that can cripple a group. At least initially, you're all working toward the same goal. If you want to be in a jazz band and the rest of your group is into heavy metal, chances are you won't be long for that group. The process that you go through in forming a band—deciding which mind-sets and personalities mesh well and which don't—should go a long way toward heading off serious problems. And make no mistake: being in a band is like being in a marriage, only it's a marriage with four or five other people involved. You get all those moods, all those personalities, and it's a wonder bands stay together for twenty days, let alone twenty years.

John Schuerholz, the former general manager of the Atlanta Braves and the man who built a dynasty in the 1990s and 2000s, has a saying about teamwork: "Gather your team. Preach them your story. If people don't get it, eliminate them." It's a blunt assessment but a correct one. If someone's not on board with what you're trying to do, no amount of pleading is going to help. And if you compromise your own aims to satisfy them, will your final product be a true reflection of your effort?

In a band, you'll understand very quickly if everybody "gets it." That's one thing that bands do very well: zoning in on a goal and executing. You can develop your "product" extremely quickly when you're together all the time. And, similarly, you should be able to handle problems in the same fashion: directly, with a minimum of attitude, scowling, and hurt feelings. Note that I said *should:* many of the most famous bands in the world are made up of players who can't stand one another off the stage. But they recognize that their greatest value is together, and they put aside their differences for the greater good—or the greater profit. The Police and the Eagles are two examples here: the supporting players have long-standing disputes with the front men of both bands, but everyone recognizes the value of working together. And there has been a payoff: both bands have put together some of the most profitable tours of recent years.

There are always going to be conflicts in a band. Some are low-level ones: the guy who always takes the choice seat in the van, the guy who bathes only once a week. But those are the kinds of issues that a bit of diplomacy can resolve.

But when success hits, the small problems can mushroom into enormous ones when matters you didn't even think were an issue suddenly flare up. That's when you need to remember what's most important—the team—and act accordingly.

In rock music as in the rest of life, the vast majority of conflicts happen because of egos. Somebody's feelings get hurt because he or she doesn't feel properly appreciated, and that person makes life miserable for everyone else around. Sometimes it's a matter of credit for work done, sometimes it's a matter of respect for effort, and sometimes (the worst case) it's about money.

You've got to address problems like this quickly and directly. If you allow them to fester, they'll tear your team apart from the inside. It's the whole ripping-the-bandage-off approach to management: speaking the truth to someone now saves a whole lot of pain, agony, and hurt feelings later.

I'll offer here the first of 38's biggest personnel challenges and the way that we dealt with them. This first conflict ended up propelling us to greater heights than we'd ever imagined. The second didn't have as happy a result.

The Sudden New Direction

The decision to take a new musical direction and step forward represented the first serious conflict we'd known in 38. Prior to that, we'd all been remarkably unified in our direction, all of us approaching life, the road, and our band in basically the same way: all for one, one for all, remaining true to one another and our Southern rock heritage. But an opportunity came along that we couldn't pass up, even if it meant that one of us had to stand on the sidelines and watch.

By late 1978, we had just about finished all the tracks for our third album when Mark Spector at A&M contacted us. An associate of his, John Kalodner, had sent him a demo tape of a song from an unknown Chicago band. Kalodner is a world-famous A&R (artists and repertoire) man, a talent scout who signed Foreigner and helped propel Aerosmith to multiplatinum heights. So when he says he's got something you ought to listen to, you put it at the top of your list.

The band was a local Chicago outfit called Survivor that hadn't had any national success. (They would go on to record the famous song "Eye of the Tiger," but that was still several years away.) The name of the song they'd written was "Rockin' into the Night," and for whatever reason, they didn't see anything in it.

Don Barnes and I, however, saw plenty. It fit in well with what we were doing; quite frankly, it was a better song than almost anything else we had on the album. It had commercial potential written all over it, and we wanted to get right back into the studio and take our shot at recording it.

And that's where the problems started.

Negotiating the Buy-In

Everybody in the band has a designated role and fits into the mix in a specific way. The drummer and bass player don't step on the guitarists' toes; the guitarists don't try to upstage the lead singer. The lead singer, in turn, is the face and voice of the band—the guy or lady everyone thinks of when they think of your band.

Our front man was Donnie Van Zant. He had the Van Zant name, which gave him and, by association, us instant credibility in the Southern rock world. He had the attitude. He had the stage presence. He had everything you could possibly want in a Southern rock front man.

The problem now was that "Rockin' into the Night" wasn't a Southern rock song. It was far more accessible, more commercial. And Donnie wasn't the greatest of singers for this kind of music. We all have our limitations, and this one was Donnie's. We didn't think he could deliver it, sell it, and make it believable. His sound was more country, more folksy, and this song demanded a vocal that was smoother, could belt, had a higher range. But Don Barnes, my fellow guitarist, had some experience as a vocalist. He'd sung in bands before joining 38.

"Man, I think I could do a good job with this one," he said, and I agreed with him, which put us in a huge dilemma because Don clearly wasn't the lead singer. But we hated the idea of missing this opportunity, so we figured we'd run the idea of Don singing the song past Donnie.

So one day in rehearsal, we played the song for Donnie. And it was clear right from the start that he wasn't feeling it. He shrugged, indifferent to the song. Don asked about the possibility of singing the song, and Donnie was fine with the idea—that is, until Rodney Mills, our producer, got hold of the song, and we all started jamming on it. At that point, it was clear we might actually have something, and suddenly Donnie decided he might want to take a crack at the song after all.

Don and I looked at each other, not sure what to do. We didn't want hard feelings, but this was our livelihood. And the stakes were high: this was most definitely our last shot. We weren't sure it was going to be a commercial success with Don, but we were almost certain it wouldn't be with Donnie.

It was do or die. But how to keep the group together without losing our front man?

This was a critical moment for all of us, and a moment that we unconsciously broke into stages:

• *Recognize when roles might shift, and be open to the possibility.* You have roles on your team for a reason. Everyone brings a different set of skills to the group, and if you've got a well-chosen group, those skills complement one another. But every so often, you'll find that one person simply doesn't have the needed expertise for a given task, even if it's a responsibility that usually falls to him or her. You can tell when someone's not right for something, but it's tricky to address. It's not a matter of assigning blame; in many cases, you're just looking for the right mix of people that current circumstances dictate.

• *Hurt feelings heal. Missed opportunities don't.* Suppose you have a sudden opportunity to meet with a key client, and your team leader is out of the office and unavailable. Should you risk postponing the meeting and discouraging the client, or should you push forward with someone else in the team leader's role? In most cases, the second answer is the correct one. The team leader needs to understand that in some cases, the greater good is more important than the pride of maintaining traditional roles.

• *If you're certain this is your best chance for success, press forward.* You have a sense of what does and doesn't work in your industry, even if it's on a general level. We knew that while a folksy Southern feel would play well in our hometown and surrounding states, it didn't play as well in Chicago, Los Angeles, or New York or any of the other parts of the country we were trying to reach. We had to decide whether we wanted to strike out into the unknown with the possibility of really breaking out, or staying in our comfort zone with the certainty that we wouldn't gain any new audience.

That day in the studio, out of respect for Donnie, we let him take a shot at the song, but it was clear to almost everyone that it wasn't working with him at the vocals. At that point, we had to say, "Sorry, man. This is the way it's going to be. You didn't like it at the beginning, and we're too far down the road to change now." Donnie didn't like the idea of being bumped aside for the song, and I can understand that. But once he put the band's dreams and plans above his own, he understood that bringing Don up to the front of the stage, at least for "Rockin' into the Night," was the best move for all of us.

> "Never call anybody out in front of the rest of the group. You take them aside, you talk to them away from everybody else. Resentments may start out small, but if not resolved, they take over the band."
> —RICKY BYRD, FORMER GUITARIST, JOAN JETT & THE BLACKHEARTS

So we recorded it as we'd planned. The song was our first Top 40 hit. We went from selling twenty-five thousand albums to selling a quarter of a million. And the voice coming out of a hundred thousand car radios in the summer of 1979 was Don's, not Donnie's.

More important, we'd made a huge commercial breakthrough. We'd recognized that there was a method to getting our songs on the radio, a method to angling both our songwriting and our singing to make it accessible to the widest possible audience. We didn't know it at the time, but we were establishing the template for our future success: Southern rock attitude, arena rock sound.

With Donnie we already had our Southern rock credentials well established; now we could start to make some commercial strides forward with Don singing. It was like discovering a completely new weapon in our arsenal, and a powerful one at that.

"Rockin' into the Night" was a critical moment for us: we had to decide what we were going to be as a band and think hard about why exactly we had gotten into this business. Obviously the first answer to that question was, "To have fun." We'd been friends growing up; we all knew we could play.

But with the money and the recognition, the question of why we did what we did started to get a bit more complex. Were we interested in creating art? Sure, but not at the expense of enjoying ourselves. Almost nobody can consciously create "art" that's any good. You express what's inside yourself, and maybe it connects with somebody else. Maybe that connection is just enough to get people to buy (or, these days, download) your song. Maybe that connection is deep enough that the song becomes a part of their lives; I still have people tell me every day how important our songs were to them as they were growing up. And maybe, if you're very lucky, that connection spreads wide, and your song becomes an anthem, a symbol of a certain moment in time. We were very lucky.

The same holds true for any business. Perhaps your product, your offering strikes enough of a chord in your customers that they'll give you a try. Perhaps it resonates deeply enough that they'll be loyal to you for a lifetime. So many people drive the same make of car or root for the same sports team for their entire lives. If you understand how to put the elements in place for that connection to possibly happen, you can greatly increase the odds that such a connection will happen.

This is not to say that you should abandon your principles and beliefs in an effort to be all things to all people. Fans, or customers, can smell pandering a mile away. In the late 1970s, one of the most popular albums around was *Saturday Night Fever*. Think we should have dropped the whole Southern rock thing and become a disco band? We could have. We were talented enough that we could play pretty much anything, and we might have even sold a couple of records.

But we would never have approached the heights that we did by building off our foundation. We were able to remain authentic to ourselves while branching off into new directions. And in that way, we could bring our old audience along with us and pick up quite a few new people along the way.

So that's the perpetual challenge that's in front of us all: balancing art and commerce. You're in business to sell your product, whatever that product may be. You deliver it in the most believable way possible, in the way that convinces your customer that your product will do the job well. And you've got to deliver on that promise; otherwise you're just a huckster. In our case, that meant putting together a complete album of quality songs, not just one or two.

I'll be the first to admit that we'd gotten a bit complacent in how to best deliver our product to our customers. We started out as a bunch of buddies, with everyone falling into their roles almost by accident.

Donnie automatically became the lead singer of our band, since his brother held the same position in Lynyrd Skynyrd. We were a de facto "Baby Skynyrd," and that's why we didn't do so well on our first two albums. Why would you want a Baby Skynyrd when you could get the full grown-up version?

But with Don, we had a new angle, and a whole new set of possibilities opened up for us. We didn't think it was a fluke, and so we didn't want to go back to the way things were before. Instead, we began writing two different kinds of songs that would suit our two different singers. Each song would hit our audience in a different place, in a different way. We had fans who loved Donnie's stuff and didn't care so much for Don's, and vice versa. But because we recognized an opportunity and acted on it, we were able to satisfy both groups and develop both faces of the band.

I don't want to say that money solves all band problems, but once we all started seeing some larger checks, we were reminded of our real purpose in this band: not to satisfy ourselves as individuals, but to please our audience and support our bandmates. By taking steps in new directions while staying loyal to our roots, we could keep everyone involved and pleased with our direction.

Verse

There may come a moment when someone on the team has to move aside for the common good. Recognize this possibility, and do what you can to minimize the hurt feelings. By the same token, understand that the good of the team is what's most important, and if you can keep everyone on board while juggling some roles here and there, you can increase opportunity across the board.

Chorus

The team is slotted into predefined roles. But imagine if you removed one member of the team. Who would step up and replace that member? And might certain team members have some hidden talents that haven't yet been allowed to flourish?

Solo

What are your own hidden talents? Do you have a knack for public speaking, or analyzing data, or organizing presentation details? Think about what you could do that you're not already doing, and you may find yourself branching out in areas you didn't expect.

8.

Just What
I Needed

Sometimes, your team needs a little outside
perspective to attack a problem. And that's when
collaboration becomes essential.

Many's the time I've left a piece of music for
dead, only to have a collaborator decide that it
wasn't so bad after all and give it new life. Or
I've hit an absolute dead end, knowing I had something
with potential but not sure how to take it to the next level,
and a collaborator would step in and say, "Switch these
parts around, put this here, that there, and add this little
piece right in there," and boom—you've got yourself a
complete song, one that's your creation with just a bit of
tweaking to make it right.

At its best, collaboration inspires both parties to create something that neither one could have done alone. I'm a huge fan of the creative advances that collaboration inspires.

Many of the greatest rock songs in history are a product of collaboration. Going all the way back to Rodgers and Hammerstein, through Leiber and Stoller (the men responsible for much of Elvis's work), to Lennon and McCartney, collaborators have an illustrious history in rock 'n' roll. Elton John is a magnificent piano player and extraordinarily creative with the keys, but it took Bernie Taupin's lyrics to turn Elton's songs into legends.

Perhaps the most famous rock music example of collaboration—not just benefiting a band, but absolutely rescuing it—happened in 1986 when Run-DMC sampled Aerosmith's 1970s hit "Walk This Way." Aerosmith had been one of America's top bands, but by the time Run-DMC came calling, the rock 'n' roll lifestyle had caught up with them, and they were shells of their former selves. Still, Run-DMC invited Aerosmith's Steven Tyler and Joe Perry to appear in the video, and they parlayed their new exposure into a series of immensely popular commercial hits. Within a few years, they were headlining the Super Bowl and, more recently, their own installment of the hit video game Guitar Hero. They succeeded beyond anyone's wildest expectations, and they owe it all to one of their own early hits.

In 38 Special, Don Barnes and I were, musically speaking, the most forward-thinking members of the band. We were the ones listening to other kinds of music, seeing how, for example, Brian May of Queen approached a song or guitar solo, or how we could tap into some of the same creative energies as the Velvet Underground or the Cars. Donnie Van Zant was writing most of our lyrics, and he wasn't straying too far afield from his Southern roots, sticking mainly to good-time party songs and girl-gone-wrong ballads.

So in a way, the stars really aligned for us in terms of bringing aboard a collaborator. Southern rock was losing its stranglehold on the radio in the late 1970s, and other forms of music were starting to take over the dial. There were so many possibilities out there. Why not bring on board a collaborator and see what we could accomplish together?

Welcoming a New Collaborator

The days after "Rockin' into the Night" broke big were exciting ones for all of us. We were starting to see the possibilities of what we could be doing with songwriting, and we couldn't wait to get back into the studio to start on our fourth album. With just one song, our entire mind-set had changed: the creation of a record wasn't a challenge but an opportunity to expand ourselves as artists. We'd made a breakthrough, and it wasn't just because we'd added Don to the lead vocal mix. We realized there was some extremely exciting music out there that wasn't limited to just our previous mainstay and comfort zone—Southern rock. We had suddenly become part of a larger universe of pop music, and we were conscious of the fact that we needed to come up with another radio-ready song.

When your first song gets played on the radio, you suddenly start paying a whole lot more attention to what's surrounding it. So that's what we began doing, absorbing everything going on around us. Opening your mind doesn't necessarily mean you're going to make better choices in songwriting, but it does mean you've got a wider range of influences and possibilities to absorb. We were sharing the charts with everyone from John Lennon to Kenny Rogers to Diana Ross, and we wanted to learn something from each of them.

One song that was all over the radio in 1979 was the Cars' hit "Just What I Needed." Bouncy, poppy, peppy, it couldn't have been further from what we were doing in the band. And I hated it. Absolutely *hated* it. I turned the channel every time it came on the radio.

But you couldn't escape that song. And before long, I'd listen to a line or two before changing the channel. Soon after that, I was listening to the whole song. And by then, it had worked its magic on me, and I, like the rest of the country at the time, loved the song.

For most of our first three albums, we'd built our sound on big, Rolling Stones–style chords and heavy Lynyrd Skynyrd–style riffs. But here was something completely different: snappy eighth notes that bounced the song right along. (A typical rock song is based on a four-count beat. Think of the "One, two, three, four!" that Paul McCartney shouts out at the start of "I Saw Her Standing There." Eighth notes are twice as fast. Count out "one-and-two-and-three-and-four-and," and every syllable is an eighth note.)

I couldn't get this rhythmic pattern out of my head, so I sat down with my guitar and started picking out a few chords. And before long, I'd come up with a cool, descending eighth-note riff that built into big, arena-rock chords. I took it to Don, who dug it and started singing a scat melody over the riff—no words, just "da-da-da-da." That's how we'd come up with the vocal melody, and we'd put the lyrics in later.

Fortunately, Don already had a title in mind for the song. He wanted it to be about a guy asking his girl to give him a little room to breathe rather than stifling him. He wanted to call it "Hold On Loosely."

Around this time, Kalodner asked if we wanted to spend some time in Chicago writing with Jim Peterick, the Survivor vet who'd written "Rockin' into the Night." Absolutely, we said. We'd love to work with Jim up close.

"My secret to being a good team player? Play with people who are better than you. It's like being a tennis player: if you play someone who stinks, you're going to be sending back weak lobs, but if you play someone who's better than you, you'll be zipping it across the net. I've always tried to work with people who force me to raise my game: Ted Nugent, Neil Schon of Journey, the guys from Aerosmith, Ozzy. These are the people who force you to get better."
—JACK BLADES, SINGER, SONGWRITER, BASSIST, NIGHT RANGER, DAMN YANKEES, SHAW/BLADES

In the course of your business, you'll have opportunities like this to work with other people on a contract basis. It's becoming far more common in today's workplace, with independent contractors and consultants becoming increasingly the norm. So if you're going to enter into one of these short-term relationships, I strongly recommend you consider the following questions as you go:

• *Who benefits?* In other words, what is the desired outcome here, and how will that benefit both parties? For us, it was a concrete goal: sit down, write a few songs together, record said songs. But if you're bringing in someone to "advise" you, "consult" with you, or offer "recommendations," proceed with a little more caution. These open-ended engagements can rapidly turn into long slogs, costing you time, money, and energy without producing easily measurable benefits.

• *Who can work well with others?* If you're bringing aboard a new teammate, that individual has a high bar to clear. You'll need him or her to be able to mesh well with the group on a day-to-day basis. A "hired gun," however, is brought aboard to provide inspiration, insight, and productivity. If you get along well on a teammate level, so much the better, but limited engagements allow you to enjoy the benefits of a pinch hitter without having to fully integrate that person into the overall team.

• *Who speaks up, and who stays silent?* One of the major problems with collaboration is that you'll end up with one alpha dog—a person who takes charge of the session and bulldozes the rest of the group with his or her ideas. It happens all the time, no matter how hard people work to prevent it. But you've got to avoid letting the alpha dog take over your collaboration. One way to do this is by requiring everyone to speak. By giving everyone the floor, even the quiet and timid members of the group, you give everyone a voice and mitigate the effect of the alpha dog.

• *Who has ownership of the final product?* This is an important consideration you should outline well before you begin. When we wrote songs with someone, we would spell out who owned what. Sometimes it was a simple process, sometimes not. (We'll cover the downside of this arrangement later.) If you're brainstorming ideas for new products, does the entire team take credit for any ideas that come up? Or do you assign ownership on a percentage basis? Sorting out the messy details beforehand can head off all kinds of problems of ownership once people decide they'd like a piece of your success.

• *What's the obligation?* Sometimes the spark just isn't there. Suppose you start working with your hired gun, and it's not clicking. You're not coming up with ideas, not breaking any new ground. What's your obligation? Can you just walk away, or are you tied to your temporary partner by contract or expectation?

Our expectations were fairly high when we met with Jim. We went to his house, and the first thing we did was thank him profusely for "Rockin' into the Night." He responded by thanking us for doing the song justice.

One of the most valuable services a collaborator can perform is finding the hidden gems in another's work. By the time we got to Jim, Don and I were down on ourselves. The commercial marketplace had made it clear it wasn't interested in what we had to offer, in the style we were presenting it. But Jim listened to what we were doing and complimented us over and over about how much he enjoyed our work. That kind of praise, from someone who's proven himself in your field, is worthwhile, because you know it's well earned.

With the mutual admiration society out of the way, we could get down to business. Jim is an outstanding lyricist and a great collaborator. And it was useful to have someone who had absorbed the same influences as us—the Beatles, the Stones, Southern rock—and yet produced work that was worlds apart from our own.

I'll never forget what happened next. As Jim's wife whipped up some nachos, we played Jim the verse, chorus, and melody line of our new song "Hold On Loosely."

"Hold on loosely," he said, searching around for some suitable accompanying lines, "but don't let go. If you cling too tightly, you're gonna lose control."

"Write that down!" Don and I said, thrilled at how fast this all seemed to be coming together. A little while later, he told us to take a walk so that he could kick around some lyrical ideas. Jim is the kind of guy whose songwriting mind is always on; he carries a note pad with him wherever he goes, and I've seen him stop conversations to hum a few notes into a pocket recorder for later use. So when he tells you to give him room, you do. And he was as good as his word: when we got back from our walk, he'd written the lyrics to the entire song. We all went out to dinner that night, celebrating the conception of what was certain to be the next great 38 Special song.

We got home from dinner, and Jim sat down at the kitchen table. He looked at the page of lyrics, set it down on the table, and scrawled a huge X right through it.

"Not good enough," he sighed.

We just about had a heart attack right there. But he told us to go to bed and sleep on it, that it would all sort itself out in the morning. And he was absolutely right. That next morning, we cranked out the lyrics, and we were ready to go. It was the first step in what would end up being a great partnership with Jim. He, Don, and I would later write "Caught Up in You," our first Top 10 hit, and "Fantasy Girl," another success.

Rocking Well with Others

At our Camp Jam events, we preach the gospel of collaboration, the keystone for any group or organization. Our camp events often bring together onstage people who have never played instruments before, forcing them to work together to rock the crowd. Collaboration isn't just a good idea; it's a do-or-die proposition.

But how do you collaborate well, so that the whole is greater than the sum of its parts?

• *Use your ears.* This one's completely obvious for anybody playing music. You've got to use your ears to play, don't you? You'd think so, but in many cases, musicians go into their own little worlds, tuning out on what the rest of the band is doing. If your drummer starts picking up the beat, it's up to you to either pay attention and keep up, or get her to slow the beat back down to the normal level. And when the time comes for you to strut your stuff, you don't want to be back in a far corner of the stage, strumming rhythm chords when you could be tearing off a screaming solo. Listening is every bit as important in the business world as it is onstage. It's vital that you pay close attention not only to what your collaborators and teammates are saying, but how they are saying it.

> "A band is only as good as its crew. You always need to look out for the people putting the show together. You've got a lazy crew, a crew that's not paying attention to the show, and everything falls apart. You need that foundation, or nothing that you do onstage matters."
> —LIBERTY DEVITTO, CAMP JAM MASTER CLASS DRUMMER AND THIRTY-YEAR VETERAN OF BILLY JOEL'S BAND

• *Use your eyes.* Onstage, collaboration isn't just about listening to what's going on around you. You've got to use your eyes too. Next time you see a band play live, watch how closely each individual keys on everyone else visually. You'll be able to identify the leader of the band fairly quickly. Sometimes it's the drummer, who controls the beat. Sometimes it's the guitarist, who runs the band like a conductor, emphasizing beats with his guitar neck. Sometimes it's the singer, who brings forward and sends back individual players with a wave of his hand.

And when you're in a team environment of your own, pay close attention to what you can see, not just what your colleagues are saying. By understanding what people are communicating with their body language as well as their words, you can develop bonds of trust that are that much stronger and that much more likely to pay off down the road. You'll know instinctively when it's your turn to step forward and when it's your turn to pull back, and your team will be that much closer to running at peak efficiency.

- *Plan ahead.* When you're collaborating, you can't just think about what you're doing now, but how what you're doing now will play in the future. You don't want to end a lyrical line with "month" or "orange"; no words in the English language rhyme with them. And you don't want to create a song for a touring band that requires three guitarists, four drummers, a keyboard player, and a full symphony orchestra to be replicated properly onstage. And speaking of onstage, you pay attention not only to what's happening at the moment, but what could be happening. Is the tempo speeding up? Is the singer screaming so loud that her voice won't last an hour? Are the roadies telling you that there's no more beer backstage? The further ahead you can see problems developing, the more likely you'll be able to head them off.

- *Take your turn in the spotlight.* Part of the thrill of being on a team is getting the chance to put the entire team on your back once in awhile and draw all the attention to yourself. For the band, it's the chance to show off your skills all alone onstage. For a team, it's the opportunity to take deserved credit for a new plan or guide through a new initiative. Everyone has something to contribute to the overall whole, and everyone should receive the proper big-time credit. The group should determine ahead of time where the solos will take place, and when the moment arrives, the group should give way to the individual.

Don and I were bouncing off the walls when we took "Hold On Loosely" to the rest of the band in the studio. You never know when a song's going to be a hit, but you do know when you've got something special. When you've got a song that everyone can't wait to play again and again, you can tell there's something going on there.

For all the hopes we had for that little song, we couldn't have possibly imagined how far it would reach. We couldn't even imagine that it would become an early 1980s anthem, let alone show up on a Guitar Hero video game a quarter of a century later.

"Rockin' into the Night" put us on the map. "Hold On Loosely" let us conquer everyone around us. With Skynyrd no longer with us, we were the ones to lead the Southern rock charge into the 1980s, and *Wild-Eyed Southern Boys,* our fourth album, was our rallying cry. It made such an enormous splash, going gold and then platinum, that to this day, people still think it's our first record.

But the album wasn't without its share of controversy. Remember the movie *Spinal Tap,* where their album *Smell the Glove* is so horribly sexist that they end up putting out an all-black album cover? We had our own *Smell the Glove* moment with *Wild-Eyed Southern Boys*. We hated every album cover that the record company came up with, but *Wild-Eyed Southern Boys* really set us off.

Next time you're in a record store or on iTunes, check out the cover. At the center is a long-legged woman wearing hot pants, her derriere taking up a good quarter of the top of the album cover. The band is standing on the front porch of a bar in the background leering at her. There're also a pickup truck, a crushed Budweiser can, a neon sign of a gun with our name across it. It's so stuffed with clichés, it's almost a parody of Southern rock. We absolutely despised the cover, thinking it represented everything we were trying to escape.

Ironically, though, that cover was probably worth a quarter million in album sales. It set off a nationwide controversy; feminist groups in the Pacific Northwest tried to have it pulled from shelves, and there were rumors of young boys entering puberty who were buying two copies! It may not have been the way we wanted to gain nationwide notice, but it sure worked.

Partly as a result of the album's notoriety, but mostly because *Wild-Eyed Southern Boys* was a collection of damn good songs, we were the support act that all the major bands wanted. Having a million-selling album will do that for you. We were in heavy demand then, touring almost constantly and playing to packed houses. We could sell five thousand to six thousand tickets a night, and that made us very attractive to bands looking to sell out arenas with eighteen to twenty thousand seats.

Those were some amazing times, and we got to know some great bands on a personal level. We opened for Rush for a few dates, and we had fun playing softball with those guys and their crew during our free time. We'd roll into town, find a park, buy some sandwiches, and break out our bats and gloves. Rush's bassist and guitarist, Geddy Lee and Alex Lifeson, were big baseball fans, but their cerebral drummer, Neil Peart, always sat in the bleachers reading a book.

"What's Neil doing?" I once asked Alex.

"Writing our next album," Alex replied.

Rush was the kind of act you like to support, because they were regular guys and understood how hard it was being a struggling band. And they showed us respect too. One of our early songs was an instrumental called "Robin Hood," and one night I was watching Rush onstage. They were at a break between songs, and as Geddy was talking to the audience, I suddenly heard the main riff to "Robin Hood" coming from somewhere. Turned out Alex was playing it softly; he looked over at me and smiled as he did it. They didn't have to treat us so well; that's just the kind of band they were.

Another band we spent a lot of time with was the Jefferson Starship, which led to one of my most memorable moments in rock 'n'roll. Although I spent a lot of time with some of the guys in the band, I never really got close to the leaders, Grace Slick and Paul Kantner. But one night while we were flying to a gig, I happened to end up in a seat next to Grace. I was in awe: a twenty-nine-year-old guitarist sitting next to a rock legend. She's an iconic figure with a great sense of humor and a very cynical view of the world. At one point, she leaned over to me and said, "Plan on being a very big band."

"Really?" I asked. "Why's that?"

"Because everybody who's opened for us has gone on to be huge. Fleetwood Mac. The Doobie Brothers. Huge." Sure enough, our career took off, though whether the Starship had anything to do with that, I can't say.

There's a funny coda to this story. Several years ago, Grace, who had retired from the music business, was touring the country as an artist. I went to her showing at an Atlanta gallery and walked up to her. "You probably don't remember me," I said, "but I spent one of the best evenings of my life with you."

"You're not Jimi Hendrix!" she replied.

She didn't recognize me, so I told her what she had said to me in that plane long ago about every opener for the Starship hitting it big.

"I never said that!" she shot back. "What ever happened to Iron Butterfly?"

Well, she had me there. But I introduced myself, and she laughed in recognition. "You were those rednecks from Florida!" she said, and I—and the crowd around us—laughed out loud as we traded story after story.

The Starship and Rush tours were all part of the growing world of 38 Special. Jim kept on collaborating with us for three albums—*Rockin' into the Night, Wild-Eyed Southern Boys,* and *Special Forces*—and then his work with Survivor started taking up the majority of his time. You can hear a bit of a shift in our sound then—not better, not worse, just different. We continued to use collaborators for the rest of my time with 38, and I think it kept the band at its best by constantly bringing in new voices to challenge us.

After the release of "Hold On Loosely" was the first time that I remember thinking that my bank account was really changing. We were making good salaries on the road, and then we started seeing checks from air-play and record sales. By this point, we were probably making seventy-five cents per record. (People see those figures and say, "Seventy-five cents a record? You sold a million records, so you guys were getting $750,000, right?" Not exactly. We had to pay the first half-million back to the record company, so we weren't getting all that money.)

Every once in awhile, though, we stepped back and thought about how far we'd come in so short a time. It was an unbelievable magnitude of change. In the space of just seven years, we went from a $2.50 per diem with nothing left over for a salary to making $1,000 a week with $40 a day in per diem, along with royalty checks that put us well into what was then the 50 percent tax bracket.

When I look back at what happened in the wake of "Rockin' into the Night" and "Hold On Loosely," it's tough to believe that the same group of guys could go from hanging out in a Jacksonville living room to flying in Gulfstream jets and performing before thousands of cheering fans. But it happens, and if it can happen to us, it can happen to anyone else.

The opportunities are always there for you, although they may not be obvious at first glance. Keep digging, keep hoping, keep working, and soon enough, you'll find yourself at a career peak, looking back and wondering at the amazing turn of events that led you to that point.

The thing is, once you're cashing checks that are more than you used to make in a year, your life starts to change—and sometimes not for the better.

Verse

Sometimes collaboration is a perfect solution. Your team may not be able to do everything on its own, and a fresh voice and perspective can help you to dust off some ideas you'd forgotten or discarded and turn them into something new.

Chorus

As a team, look at yourselves and judge yourselves honestly: What are your holes? Where do you need the most work? What areas of your industry do you not have adequately covered? What areas have you covered so thoroughly that you can't find anything new? These are the places to target with consultation and collaboration.

Solo

Think of yourself as a collaborator. What do you have to offer another team? What are your key skills? Is it possible you're not using them to greatest effect with your own team? Reassess frequently what your strengths are and how you've developed those strengths since your last self-assessment.

9

A Change Is Gonna Come

HURT FEELINGS are a NORMAL PART OF ANY BUSINESS. BUT IF THEY SIMMER AND TURN INTO RESENTMENT, THAT'S WHEN THE REAL TROUBLE BEGINS, PARTICULARLY WHEN MONEY IS INVOLVED.

e in 38 Special were a fortunate bunch of guys for any number of reasons. So much had to go so right for us so many different times, and it did. We broke big because of the contributions and assistance of numerous people who were willing to take a chance on us. And we tried not to lose sight of that. We really tried.

We weren't the kind of band that squabbled over every little thing. Some bands, like the Black Crowes and Oasis, actually have fistfights with one another.

(Of course, both of those bands are fronted by pairs of brothers, so that might have something to do with it.) We were basically a go-along-to-get-along bunch of guys. It may not have made for great tabloid headlines, but it kept us pretty happy.

We were also in a position to start helping bands lower down on the ladder than we were. Back around 1986, a hot young New Jersey band by the name of Bon Jovi began opening for us. We hit it off with them almost immediately, and I'm still friends with them. We didn't stay in the same hotels in every city, but when we did, we'd meet up with Jon Bon Jovi and his drummer, Tico Torres, and play poker. It didn't matter if there was a wild party going on around us; we'd bust out those cards.

Bon Jovi also provided us with an object lesson in the changing nature of popular tastes. It was on that tour that we first realized that our ride wouldn't last forever. We were coming back from a successful show and walking from the bus through the hotel lobby. A few women spotted us, shrieked, and came running over. (Never a bad sign, right?)

We all piled into an elevator together, and the women were nearly breathless with excitement. "You guys are 38 Special, aren't you?" they asked.

We puffed up our chests a bit. "Why, yes we are," we replied.

"Great!" they said. "Do you know what room Bon Jovi is in?"

Ouch.

When Love Meets Money

The realization that our road might have an end to it wasn't the only hurdle we faced. About the time we started making real money, we began seeing the potential for problems. We tried our best to be equitable in how we broke down our income. Everybody shared evenly in the artists' royalties from record sales and the touring. That was the correct thing to do; we were all members of a team, and the team couldn't function with any of us absent. You could argue over the relative value of, say, the lead singer versus the bass player, but that wasn't an argument we were interested in having. We were a team, and we shared the revenue from all actions involving the entire team in equal percentages.

Where things got tricky was when we started to apportion out royalties for songwriting. We had set up our own publishing company and drawn up partnership and shareholder agreements to do our best to head off any uncertainty. But when you're dealing with creativity, something that by definition can't be measured, there's nothing but uncertainty.

Songwriting is a competitive business, with every element of the process a competition, right down to whose name comes first in the credits. For decades, Rolling Stones songs were credited exclusively to "Jagger/Richards." Mick and Keith didn't let anyone else in on the songwriting aspect of the band. Led Zeppelin took the ethically questionable approach of "adapting" old blues songs and giving themselves "credit" as song-writers; years later, they would add the original blues artists to the credits to ensure they received proper financial and songwriting benefits.

Certainly there's ego involved in these sorts of conflicts. But much more important, it's about the money. Songwriters can make much more money off the licensing rights to their songs than they can through any other role in the band. It's why you continue to see classic rock songs show up in commercials: the songwriters make phenomenal amounts of money off the use of those songs, and obviously the songs hold value long after the band has either broken up or lost its headlining status. Standard publishing agreements in music call for royalties to be split fifty-fifty between the songwriter and the "publisher."

Sometimes the publisher is the songwriter's company, meaning the songwriter gets all the royalties, and sometimes the publisher is someone completely different—a manager perhaps. The music industry is filled with sad stories of musicians who assigned their "publishing" rights to underhanded types who took a huge cut of the profits of many of music's most popular songs.

The Beatles are an especially good case study here. In 1963, along with their manager and a music publisher, they created Northern Songs, a publishing company that held their publishing rights. But the Beatles quickly began earning so much money from every side—song-writing, record sales, touring, and so on—that they were paying out more than 90 percent of their money in taxes. (England's tax laws are so oppressive that the very wealthy often choose to spend a majority of the year outside the country to dodge the regulations. That's why the Rolling Stones entitled one album *Exile on Main Street*.)

Unfortunately, the Beatles were victimized by some extremely poor managerial decisions. In England, capital gains are taxed at a far lower rate than straight income, and thus Northern Songs went public on the London Stock Exchange in 1965. But because of the structure of the contracts setting up the company, Lennon and McCartney didn't have veto power over the company's direction. Moreover, each held only 15 percent of the shares, and George Harrison and Ringo Starr held 1.6 percent between them.

Worst of all, the Beatles had no right of first refusal should the other partners in Northern Songs ever wish to sell their interest, and so they had to watch as the most lucrative publishing catalogue in the history of the world passed from hand to hand that wasn't their own. Several buyout bids later, the rights to the songs in the Northern Songs catalogue ended up with Michael Jackson and, later, Sony. That's why you can hear Beatles music selling pizza and cars today.

The Beatles problem is not one that you or I are likely to ever have, but that doesn't mean you shouldn't prepare for the possibility of success. As I've stressed over and over, make sure you've got people looking out for your interests and that they benefit only *after* you do. (Agents, for instance, typically take a 15 percent cut of your earnings; they earn their fee by making sure you're in a position to earn anything at all. If they don't work, you don't work, and they don't earn.)

And while the last thing you want to see is a wedge driven between team members, it's worth remembering that at some points, you do have to look out for yourself. As a songwriter, you're always keeping an eye on how many songs you've got in development for a given record. If you're falling behind, you start to think, *Hey, I better write another song* or *I need to push a little harder for mine to get on here to even things up.*

Every band—every team—has a different makeup. Some are a meritocracy, meaning whoever comes up with the best tune gets the credit. Others are star driven, with one or two leaders getting the lion's share of the songwriting credit. But no matter what the team, if the band doesn't divide up all revenues in an equal fashion, there's bound to be resentment.

All Band Members Are Not Created Equal

It's my opinion that a band shouldn't be an equal relationship, but I'm coming from the point of view of a songwriter. The songwriter has a special skill when it comes to creating music. The other guys in the band are making very good livings playing the drums or the bass or something else, but they're making those livings because of the people writing the songs. I don't see that there should be resentment there, but then, I wasn't one of those guys.

The division between songwriters and nonsong-writers is a pretty clear one. It's not too tough to tell if somebody is or isn't in the room when you're writing a song. Where it gets tricky is when divisions start to form between the songwriters.

A typical songwriting arrangement works like this. Let's say you and I sit down to write a song together. We grab a guitar, a pen, and a pad of paper and start working out the basics: the chord structure, the theme, the verse and chorus, the vocal melody line. And before long (we hope), we've got ourselves a basic song. Now obviously that song will be sweetened and improved by our bandmates in the studio; they will take a piece of music and add their own unique stamp to it, branding it as the band's. But that song fundamentally begins with you and me in that room.

As a result, in most cases, you and I would split the songwriting fifty-fifty. If there were three of us in the room, we'd split it into thirds. It's not overly complicated. Although there could be millions of dollars at stake, there probably aren't, and you don't want to scuttle the future for the sake of a few speculative percentage points. You want to reward people for their work. We've given a percentage of a song for anyone who writes the perfect bridge. (The bridge is the section of the song that's a slight departure from the original tune musically and lyrically. In "Hold On Loosely," for example, it's the part that goes, "Don't let it slip away, sentimental fool." It's a tangential thought that prepares the listener for the return of the original riff of the song, and it can be tricky to compose.) We've even given people 10 percent of a song if they come up with a great title.

The basic idea, then, is to reward people for their effort and recognize distinctive contributions. But around 1986, when we were regularly going platinum with our albums and bringing in large royalties, we started to see the first friction in the songwriting process. One of the guys started saying, "Well, you wrote 21.33 percent of this song, and I wrote 42.5 percent, so my percentage of the royalties needs to be higher." How do you even figure that? It was crazy; it got to the point that we were fighting over whether one guy had written a certain word.

This is the kind of problem that destroys organizations. The rules of the game shift, whether by circumstance or because of one player, and suddenly everyone loses their bearings. As with everything else in a team environment, it comes down to communication, or the lack thereof. But you as an individual also need to keep a constant eye on the dynamic within your team so that you can head off these problems as quickly as possible:

• *Recognize when you're entering unfamiliar territory.* Be aware of when circumstances are changing around you. Having an equal royalty split was just fine when we weren't making a whole lot of money. But when the difference between 30 percent of a song's royalties and 32 percent is significant, someone will take notice. Similarly, when success is on the horizon for you, take the time to consider how it will affect everyone on your team. How will credit be divvied up? Will everybody be receiving rewards equivalent to their contributions to the whole? And if not, is that going to cause problems in your team? Only you know the personality and work habits of your team, but if you can see that there are potential problems down the line, you need to address them *now*.

• *Keep everyone on the same page.* Letting people know the potential for a problem and solving that problem are two different things, of course. But airing the possibility that there could be difficulty—or, to phrase it more positively, "What are we going to do when we're a huge success?"—lets everyone on your team know that you're concerned with the ongoing success of the team and you're responsive to concerns. Nothing is more damaging to a team than a member who feels slighted but has nowhere to turn; that's a recipe for disaster within the team. Resentment fuels resentment, and if your team begins dividing into factions, you're not going to have a team for much longer.

• *Agree to revisit the issue.* So the success hits, you've got your plan, and all's good. Right? Of course not. Your previous management structure may have been a reliable arrangement that you could implement and forget about; we operated under the same rules for twelve years before they became an issue. But there's an old saying: the only thing that's constant is change. You've got to revisit your solutions time and again to make sure they still work for the changing environment of your business. Success is a nice problem, but it can rapidly become a nightmare if not handled properly.

Too many musicians pay too little attention to their finances. They say: "I don't want to worry about money. I just want to write songs and play music." Poring over balance sheets and reading audit statements certainly isn't as sexy as playing guitar in front of a sold-out crowd, but doing one allows you to do the other.

We were pretty diligent in trying to track our money. I was always grateful for the education that I had received that allowed me to look at more than just what was right in front of my face. I wasn't too stubborn or too ignorant to understand when somebody was giving me good advice. But that wasn't always the case with some of my bandmates, as you'll see in a moment.

There was a bond of trust between us and our accountants, and it was because of the way that they taught us to take care of ourselves. They showed us the benefits of quarterly accounting and brought us up to speed in a hurry on the need to audit our record company.

"Audit the record company?" we'd ask. "Why do we need to do something like that?"

"Remember the time you went to LA and they had a limo pick you up?" our accountants would reply. Indeed we did; nothing makes you feel like a big shot faster than getting into a limo in Los Angeles.

"Well, who do you think paid for that limo?"

"The record company, of course."

Guess again. They showed us that we were actually paying for our own limo, among many other little things we'd never imagined were counting against us. And all of a sudden, we realized we actually did have to stay on top of this stuff.

Our accountants also tried to drill the value of saving into our heads. There are many different ways to save your money, and our accountants spent a lot of time demonstrating these ways to us. And they drilled one overriding lesson into our heads: there's no such thing as not paying taxes. You can have tax shelters and you can defer your income, but whatever you do, you're going to have to pay taxes. So since you can't flee to another country and avoid taxes like the Beatles did, you need to reduce your tax liability.

They were trying to get us to understand that in a year, all our success could be nothing but a pleasant memory. There was no guarantee that we'd stay at the top of the charts for another year, much less another decade.

Back then, the tax rate was 50 percent. That's quite a bite, but with a bit of savvy investing, we were able to create some individual nest eggs and save for our retirement while deferring (and, to some extent, reducing) the huge tax hit.

You'd think this was a clear good idea, but not everyone saw it that way. One guy in our band heard that 50 percent tax rate fact and absolutely hit the roof: "Nobody's going to tell me what to do with my money. I'll pay my tax, and I'll do what I want with the rest." The accountants tried patiently to explain to him that setting up a retirement account would ultimately result in the government's subsidizing 50 percent of every dollar he put in there, but he wouldn't hear of it.

That would be fine—shortsighted and ultimately devastating, but fine—if he were an individual and not part of the corporation that was 38 Special. But his focus on today rather than tomorrow kept us from taking advantage of some corporate financial advantages and ended up hurting everybody on the team to one degree or another. We had set up 38 with the stipulation that everyone had to agree on major decisions like this, and obviously everyone didn't agree.

Of course, certain teams do extraordinarily well. When you've got a band like a Bon Jovi, which has sold 100 million CDs, there's less reliance on your bandmates and a lot more on your own business team. Everybody fortunate enough to be in those kinds of situations becomes a minicorporation within the corporation.

The Green-Eyed Monster

The problems that can divide a band start with that green-eyed monster, jealousy. Our accountants came up with what they thought was a useful tool, a spreadsheet demonstrating how all the publishing royalties were split up among all the members of the band. It was a complex process but also a logical one. They had broken down what each guy would be making based on what percentage of songs he'd written and how successful those songs were. The guy who writes a hit makes a lot more than the guy who writes a B-side that never gets anywhere near a radio.

But it's impossible to determine what song will be a hit and what won't. Sure, you can make guesses—the tune with the killer hook and soaring chorus has a better chance than the slow, ponderous bass-driven dirge—but there's nobody who can reliably create major hits year in and year out. And it takes just as much work to create a B-side as it does a hit. You spend the same amount of time rehearsing, working through alternatives, syncing up the lyrics and the music, figuring out enhancements like the bridge and guitar solo. For whatever reason, though, some songs strike the proverbial chord with the audience, and some vanish into the deep water without even making a ripple.

But try telling that to the guy who poured his heart and soul into the song that's buried deep in the album (somewhere on Side 2, back when records had sides). He busted his back end to create his song and convinced the rest of the band to buy into his vision. And now he's seeing one or more of his bandmates reaping huge rewards because their songs, not his, happened to hit big. He can express his frustration, but the truth is, the most popular songs generate multiple revenue streams—everything from airplay on multiple stations to commercials to, these days, ring tones—and those fortunate songwriters deserve the rewards.

When a lot of money is involved, you start hearing, "Yeah, but what about me?" more and more. And when individuals start putting themselves above the team, you can count on troubles coming soon.

Financial situations vary wildly, and we're not here to teach you how to handle your money. But based on the way that so many rock stars have ended up either bankrupt or still living tour to tour, paycheck to paycheck, we can tell you this: while you ought to run your business like a rock star, you probably shouldn't run your finances like one.

Verse

When money and credit enter the picture, a team can find itself fracturing quickly. Handshake agreements aren't enough; you've got to have your deals in writing, and you've got to abide by those deals. Set down an equitable arrangement as soon as possible, and make sure everyone understands the expectation that they adhere to that arrangement—and the costs if they don't.

Chorus

As a team, decide how credit and money, if applicable, will be spread among the team before you take on a new project. Recognize that effort and outcome are entirely separate, and make sure that everyone on the team understands that. Go over the parameters of the agreement as often as possible to ensure everyone stays on the same page as long as possible.

Solo

Take some time to value your own activities. What kind of value would you place on your skills? Are you at or above the level of your peers and competitors? What *do you consider fair compensation and credit? Are you willing to accept a split arrangement with others, or do you expect credit proportional to effort? Thinking about your value ahead of time makes negotiation easier, since you already know what to ask for and what to expect.*

So You Wanna Be a Rock 'n' Roll Star

DELIVER YOUR MESSAGE WITH AUTHORITY, VOLUME, AND A HEALTHY DOSE OF ATTITUDE.

here's a reason everybody wants to be a rock star. The fame, the applause, the rock lifestyle—that's all part of it, of course. But it all boils down to that moment when you walk onstage to a sea of screaming fans, everyone there to see you. It's a rush I can't even begin to describe in words. You may not ever have the chance to get onstage in front of thousands of people screaming your name, but you can prepare all the same to deliver your own message with the voice, authority, and attitude of the best rock stars.

One of the questions people always ask me is, "Do you ever get nervous before you go onstage?" In the early days, absolutely. We were terrified back then. We were walking into a situation we'd never been in before, and it's an experience that's quite frightening. That's why we all clung together on the stage when we were opening for Peter Frampton: we were instinctively sticking with what we knew, which was staying within arm's reach of each other.

Stage fright is real, and some musicians won't tour because they don't feel at ease onstage; they'd rather connect with their audience from a distance. Nevertheless, the vast majority of musicians get used to being in front of an audience. We understand that sometimes we'll look foolish and sometimes we'll embarrass ourselves, but for the most part, we learn how to deal with and eventually master the butterflies in our stomach. It's like driving a car: you were terrified the first time you had to think about merging onto the interstate; now you do it with ease.

The further along we went in our career, the less the idea of going onstage bothered us, and part of it was the confidence that we had when we were holding our instruments. It didn't take long for us to get comfortable playing bars, or clubs, or arenas, or stadiums, and once we were comfortable, there was no stopping us.

Whether we were the opening act or the headliner, we went out there to kill. We might like the band we were on the bill with, we might hang out with them before the show or party with them afterward. But when we got onstage, it was take-no-prisoners, and most bands intuitively understand that.

The fear of going onstage, of getting up before an audience, is perfectly understandable. We fear looking stupid more than we fear just about anything else on earth. At Camp Jam, we see this all the time: people who aren't used to being in the limelight suddenly freeze up at the thought of having to get onstage in front of their peers and bosses. We do our best to tell them it's okay to feel a little fear, that fear is healthy; it shows you're taking things seriously. But we also counsel them with a bit of advice that runs along these lines:

- *Know your job.* Everyone's had the dream that you're back in school and you've got a final exam that you didn't study for. It's the fear of a lack of preparation, the fear that you didn't do enough to get the job done. But if you know exactly what you're supposed to be doing—if you rehearse that quarterly earnings report, if you know the contents of your PowerPoint inside and out, backward and forward—you won't be caught unprepared there up onstage.
- *Trust in your teammates.* This one is huge, almost as important as your own preparation. You've got to have faith that your team will get the job done, and you get that faith by seeing your team in action. Prepare, prepare, prepare. If your group has to present findings to a client, brainstorm every alternative. Build confidence up, and never tear it down. Faith feeds on faith, and if one person believes that you can deliver a first-rate performance, everyone will believe it. Also make sure you don't

limit yourself to just knowing your own share of the presentation. If one of your teammates fumbles, you want to be there to pick him or her up. Onstage, musicians have to deal with all kinds of unexpected problems: your strings might break, your amps might blow out, your bass player might get hit in the head with a beer bottle. If someone's not ready to step in and cover for a bandmate, the entire song could fall apart in an instant.

• *What's the worst that could happen?* In only rare cases—a critical briefing of your CEO, a job interview—will your performance be a do-or-die affair. And in those cases, it's essential to prepare for every possibility. But in most instances, if you stumble over your words or—heaven forbid—fall off the stage, the only thing hurt will be your pride. And that will make for a better story than even a perfectly delivered presentation! All that you've got at risk is your pride.

• *Start small.* If you dropped someone with no experience with crowds in front of a packed, twenty-thousand-seat arena, that poor soul might fall into a fetal position right there onstage. That's why you build up to the big moment, getting comfortable in front of two people, then twenty, then two hundred. Get your confidence up in front of friendly crowds before heading into the unknown.

• *Be whoever you want to be.* When we're doing our Camp Jam gatherings, it never fails that someone who was quiet and shy when starting out blossoms into someone who dominates the stage. It's an amazing transformation, but as people get more comfortable with their guitar or their microphone, they start shedding their old personality like shaking off an old coat. They're free up there on stage, free to be the wild rock star they've always dreamed of being. Onstage, the old rules don't apply. You're a new you. (That's not to say you should cap off your sales presentation with some explosions and a dive into the seats. But a little flash and flair, or just a bit more confidence, will do wonders for your public image.)

• *Do it.* Go ahead and get up there. You can sit in the wings, waiting to get the courage up to get out in front of the world—or the sales team—but like getting adjusted to a chilly pool, the best thing to do is to just dive right in. What have you got to lose?

The Moment the Lights Go Out

By the time we were at our peak in the mid-1980s, we didn't fear going onstage anymore. We were playing about two hundred shows a year, and although each one had its own charms, all had something in common: when the preconcert music snapped off in the middle of a song, the crowd would start screaming, knowing what was about to come. And then when the lights went off, the noise rattled the roof. That was the moment we waited for, the moment when we were walking out onto the stage, instrument in hand, knowing we were preparing to do what we were born to do. And then the lights come up, and it's all about you and your team. You're there together with a crowd at your feet. It's a feeling you can't describe, but it's an unbelievable sense of power. A crowd is cheering your every word: all you have to do is say the name of their city to drive them wild. That's when you feel that you could get them to do anything, and it's a tremendous rush.

The further along that went, the more we were able to play the crowd. We could break out "Rockin' into the Night," "Hold On Loosely," "Fantasy Girl," "Caught Up in You," and so many other songs, every single one guaranteed to bring the crowd to its feet.

There were more than a few times that we were exhausted coming to the arena. We'd stayed up too late the night before, maybe had too much to drink, or something else, and we were all going, "Aw, man, I'm never going to do that again. Just let me get through this show." And then the lights go down, the stage lights come up, and it's as if someone has shot a huge syringe of adrenaline right into you. We've had some of our best shows that way.

Why? Who knows? Maybe if you're not focusing too much on the gig, you don't have time to get nervous or think about the mistakes you made the night before. Although I would never recommend you tie one on before a critical presentation of your own, I can tell you that it's a good idea not to constantly focus on the big moment.

That's why preparation is so important. If you're ready for your moment in the spotlight, if you know your speech or your presentation cold or are prepared for your debate, then you're going to be just fine if anything crops up to take you off course.

Surviving a Life in Rock 'n' Roll

We'd be lying if we said we didn't live the rock 'n' roll lifestyle. We did the kinds of things that you've heard about that you probably wouldn't want your kids imitating. But for whatever reason, the way we were raised or the way we'd worked our way up from the trenches, we never let the lifestyle control us the way it controlled, and claimed, so many of rock's finest.

We were always observing other bands to take lessons from them, and when it came to the rock 'n' roll lifestyle, a lot of what we took away was what *not* to do. We saw major artists have to be carried onstage. They would perform terribly, cruise on past glories, and not give their audiences their money's worth.

Say what you will about hedonism or self-indulgence or whatever you want to call it, but look at it from the perspective of fans. They've waited for this night for weeks. They've spent their hard-earned money on your albums and on a ticket. They've talked about it with their friends, they've battled traffic to get to the arena, they've listened as the local radio station plays your songs over and over all afternoon to get the city pumped for the show. Now they're in their seats, waiting in the arena for you to come onstage. They've devoted their time and money to you. And now you're going to give them a terrible show because you couldn't control yourself? How unprofessional is that?

I don't know whether you can call the way we approached our music a "Southern thing," but I do know there was something that ran through all of the major Southern bands. Skynyrd and the Allman Brothers had this spirit to them—something that wouldn't let them put on a bad show no matter how much damage they'd done the night before. Other bands didn't take their job as seriously; they'd think of a rock tour not as a job, but as a favor they were doing to their audience. To us, that was just disrespectful. I remember seeing other bands fall off the edge and thinking, *I don't want to do that. I don't want to end up the way those guys are.*

It's disappointing seeing some of your idols and friends like that, but there's a lesson here: when you're observing the way someone approaches his or her work, don't just look at what this person is doing; consider how the public receives his or her work. For us, that meant not just watching these guys stumbling around onstage; it meant looking out into the audience as well. We'd see these looks on people's faces: they wanted to be enjoying themselves,

"When I was a kid, I stood in line for three hours to see The Who. And then, twenty years later, I'm playing with Roger Daltrey. He's spinning his mike, and it's whizzing right by my head. I get a chill talking about it. . . . The moment that it becomes all about the money, the moment you stop doing it for love of music, you've lost your way, and it ain't easy finding your way back."
—RICKY BYRD, FORMER GUITARIST, JOAN JETT & THE BLACKHEARTS

and yet a part of them knew they were getting a raw deal when the band couldn't keep itself together.

So keep an eye on the competition's customers as well. What are they saying about your competitor's performance? If you, say, run a restaurant, read the reviews and comments on other restaurants in your area. If you run a customer service–oriented business, pay attention to the complaints your customers are lodging about your competitors. The Internet gives everybody a voice, and plenty of people use it to vent about everything under the sun. If you see people complaining over and over about, say, a restaurant's poor service or surly waiters or dirty restrooms, or whatever the equivalent might be in your own business, make certain that your service is first rate, your waiters greet your customers with a smile, and your restrooms are gleaming. It's not just about putting on the best performance you can; it's knowing where the other guy is falling short and exploiting those weaknesses. The faster you gain a reputation as a customer-friendly operation that delivers the goods reliably, the better off you're going to be with your customers.

Now, all of this talk about responsibility and dedication to your customer might make it seem as if we were a group of choirboys. Not quite, trust me! We partied plenty. But we didn't party every night. We took our job too seriously for that. We also saw people die from traveling too far down the other path, and that wakes you up in a hurry. There was a period in the mid-1980s when we really tore it up; I think that lasted for maybe a tour, a tour and a half. But at some point, we pulled it back and realized we needed to get a bit of perspective and think long term, not just how to get our rush for the next night.

I think one of the main reasons we stayed so grounded was that we weren't an out-of-the-box success. It took us years of hard work to reach the heights we did. If we'd screwed around early on, as many bands did, I can't imagine we'd have had the dedication to stick it out through the rough times so that we could eventually enjoy the good ones.

The lesson here is an obvious one: always be preparing for a larger stage. Don't get lost in the roar of a crowd, particularly if that crowd is your equivalent of a club gig. Early on, we heard plenty of cheers, but a lot of it was because of the songs we were playing—covers of famous songs by artists far more popular than we were. But if we'd let ourselves fall in love with the cheers of a crowd of two hundred people, we'd never have learned what we needed to know to make that crowd grow to twenty thousand.

Verse

The crowd can carry you to the heights, but it can also bring you back down in a hurry. Make sure you're prepared for the crowds, be they people observing a presentation or the "crowds" who are your customers. Remember that old line about never getting a second chance to make a first impression, and be prepared to go to battle every time you hit the stage.

Chorus

Rehearse, rehearse, rehearse! Always prepare for your next gig. Work together to get your team prepared for the stage, and never lose sight of the fact that all the work you do offstage is just buildup to that time when you're in front of a crowd.

Solo

Public speaking is one of the most terrifying things a person can do, but there's no reason you can't get over your fear. Take every opportunity you can to speak in front of crowds, starting with friendly ones and moving forward from there. You may wish to take a class in public speaking, or you might want to throw yourself in the deep end and go to a karaoke bar. Whichever you do, keep in mind that the only thing you're risking is your pride, and that heals more quickly than you think.

New Kid in Town

Bringing in a new key member isn't easy, but sometimes it's the only way to keep the team alive.

At some point, every music fan will see his or her favorite band break up. Particularly if you're a teenager, the pain is like losing a family member, and you go through all the stages of grief, from denial ("No! The Police can't be breaking up! It's not happening!") to bargaining ("Please just stay together. Any Led Zeppelin is better than no Led Zeppelin.") to acceptance ("Guess I'll be buying a lot of solo albums now."). As a fan, I would always wonder what could possibly lead bands to break up when they had such a good thing going. As a former rock star, I can tell you exactly what leads to breakups and, I hope, help you head off a nasty split of your own.

Taking a step backward to take a step forward, how do you critique your team's performance? I don't mean "criticize"; "critique" takes a more impartial, not necessarily negative, look at your team's performance. Do you perform regular self-evaluations? Do you wait until your superior steps in and points out your flaws? Or do you just cruise onward, dealing with problems as they arise?

There are plenty of ways to handle self-evaluation, but it needs to be done, and done on a regular basis. Everybody slips, everybody backslides, and everybody has an off night now and then. There's nothing wrong with that as long as you recognize it and address it appropriately.

Probably our biggest problem as a band was the difficulty that we had in these kinds of self-evaluations. We were always attentive to detail, paying close attention to what we were doing onstage as well as what everyone around us was doing. We'd take time after every show to break down our performance and think about what we could do better. Maybe the tweaks were as subtle as standing a few steps over, and maybe they were major, like reworking an arrangement on a song. But we tried to resolve them before they became major problems.

Nevertheless, if you look hard enough, you can find flaws in every performance, and there was one guy in our band who did just that. Nothing was ever good enough for him; he found problems in even the most flawless of performances. We'd come offstage having just rocked twenty thousand people, and he'd be griping about one thing or another every single night. Certainly we weren't perfect; like anybody else, we had off nights. We knew when we weren't playing up to our potential and didn't have that fire in our belly. But to be told night after night how we were falling short as a band is wearying.

Criticism is a dangerous weapon. Used properly, it can be a great motivator, helping people really understand where they need to make improvements and strengthen the team as a whole. But looking for the flaws and focusing on them to the exclusion of any praise is extremely dangerous for any business. The trick is balance: focusing on solutions, not just problems. Here are several positive approaches to criticism that encourage improvement and keep morale high:

- *Don't be afraid to criticize.* Constant praise is almost as bad as constant criticism. Sure, everyone loves praise, but it's like eating cotton candy at every meal. At some point, you need a good serving of broccoli. Otherwise you're never going to improve, and you'll keep making the same mistakes because you thought you were doing the right thing. Even worse is when you know you're falling short yet you're still receiving praise: that leads you to devalue the praise entirely. So whether you're assessing your own performance or that of your teammates, make sure you don't skim over the negative side of the analysis just to preserve somebody's feelings. In the long run, the outcome will be better.

• *Don't be afraid to praise.* But don't go so far in your criticism that you fail to hand out praise where it's due. You'd be amazed at how difficult it is for some people to praise others. But a bit of praise is essential in order to get criticism taken seriously; otherwise you risk the opposite extreme of the situation above: nobody takes your criticism seriously because that's all you do. Everybody does something right every day just by getting through the day. Find that positive element, and be sure to highlight it.

• *Be honest in your self-evaluation.* There's nothing more toxic to a team environment than the person who criticizes everyone else's performance but has no harsh words for his or her own. Not only is it completely disruptive to team morale; it's completely wrong. Everyone makes mistakes, everyone needs to take the time to analyze what he or she is doing wrong. One individual's performance isn't the baseline; it's the team's overall performance that matters, and everyone needs to measure themselves against the ideal.

• *The criticism isn't the end product; improvement is.* All too often, criticism is its own end, giving someone a chance to vent frustrations without thinking of the long-term consequences or opportunities. But the idea with criticism is (or at least should be) helping to improve everyone's game so that the entire team is working at a higher level. "You were terrible!" is useless, damaging criticism. "You were terrible, but here's what you can do to improve" may not be the most effective approach, but it's at least got that component of advice. "This could be

better, and here's how," is a less blaming, more construc-
tive approach.

We could have used a little advice on how to handle
our own situation. I never could understand it. We were
absolutely on top of the world: making money, traveling
the world, playing to sold-out arenas and adoring fans. We
should have been having fun, and yet one band member
still wasn't happy. And his unhappiness was making the
rest of us miserable.

Constant negativity wears anyone down. You start
to think less of yourself and less of your team, and it's
not hard to fall into the trap of thinking that everything
you're doing is substandard.

At some point in a bad relationship, you have to
say, "It's not worth it. This has been a good long run, but
I've got to call it a day." It actually got to the point that one
of my bandmates and I decided we were going to bolt
right in the middle of the tour: go back to the hotel, book
a flight, and that would be it. Fortunately, we got talked
out of that one and decided to take a different approach.

There were some real ironies in the fracturing of
the band. One was that the bandmate who was so harsh
was Don Barnes, whose vocals had given us a whole
new angle to our music. He'd opened many doors for
us, and now he was starting to close them with his way
of approaching the band. So we sat down with him and
talked it out. He'd always wanted to do a solo album,

and we all figured that perhaps this was the best opportunity for him to do that.

One More Shot at the Brass Ring

After Don left, we needed a new lead singer to complement Donnie, and as luck would have it, our manager gave us a demo tape of a band called Jack Mack & The Heart Attack, produced by Glenn Frey of the Eagles. Jack Mack's lead singer, Max Carl, had a style and a sound that we thought would fit in well with 38. I invited him to Atlanta to talk about opportunities, and when he got off the plane, he was wearing Bermuda shorts and a hat with a big feather on it. Plus, he's six-foot-four, so it's not as if he wasn't drawing attention anyway. *Oh boy,* I thought, *here we go.*

But as it turned out, Max was an ideal bandmate. He had a powerful voice and a real feel for both music and lyrics. That led to the second irony surrounding Don's departure. On our first album with Max, *Rock & Roll Strategy,* we wrote and recorded a song called "Second Chance." Max sang the song and wrote some of the lyrics, and it became our biggest hit ever, going all the way to number 2. And Don had fought against this same song for years.

A lot of people, Don included, didn't feel that "Second Chance" was really a "38 song." I never distinguished among songs that way. Sure, we weren't going to be doing any opera or hip-hop. But if a song hit me a certain way, if I thought we could do it justice and make something lasting, I'd push for giving it a try. (Even so, to this day when the name 38 Special comes up, nobody says "Second Chance"! It was our biggest hit, but people always think of "Hold On Loosely" or "Caught Up in You" first.)

"Second Chance" ended up having a special meaning for us as a band as well. With Don gone, there was every possibility that we could have just folded up our tents and packed it in. He was the pop voice of 38 Special, and without him, we'd lost one of our key weapons. But we brought in Max, and all of a sudden, we were at heights we had never reached before. We were touring radio stations, and everywhere we went, people told us that phones were ringing off the hook to request that song.

At the end of 1989, I was invited to an ASCAP (American Society of Composers, Authors, and Publishers) dinner honoring the fifty most played songs of the previous year. My wife and I were seated at a table with Rod Stewart and Bruce Hornsby, among others. The presenters counted down from the fiftieth most played song of the year to the first, and I assumed I'd be up and done within the first five minutes. But "Second Chance" ended up the ninth most played song of that year.

Who would have expected that after more than a decade together, we could bring in a new key member and enjoy even more success? It's the rare band that can pull off that kind of feat; ironically, one of the few that did so was also making a lead singer transplant at the same time we were. Van Halen had built its reputation on the party-rock attitude of singer David Lee Roth, but when egos skyrocketed, the band replaced him in 1985 with Sammy "I Can't Drive 55" Hagar. With Hagar, the band hit number 1 on the pop charts, something it had never done with Roth, and pulled off the neat trick of establishing a completely new identity under the same name. (Tensions grew once again, however, setting off a revolving door of lead singers in the band.)

Losing even a key member of your team isn't always the kiss of death. Almost everyone is replaceable to some degree, although it will almost certainly mean your team has a strikingly different identity. The key to such a dramatic shift, however, is determining why that key member left—whether it was the team's fault or the member's—and making the appropriate accommodations and changes to keep the team alive and functioning on its highest possible level.

We were extremely fortunate that things worked out as well as they did, but we already had in place a mind-set that allowed the possibility of a successful "singer transplant." Based on what we went through, I have this advice for anyone needing to replace an essential member:

• *Keep your mind open to all possibilities.* The tendency is to find someone similar to the person you're replacing. But you might find the perfect replacement in someone younger or someone of a different gender. Max Carl was from Nebraska, a far cry from Jacksonville, but he fit in immediately with the new style of music we were looking to play. Other bands have taken the opposite tack; Journey, Judas Priest, and Boston replaced their singers with unknowns who had been singing the band's hits in a tribute band. (Talk about your dream come true: one day you're touring bars playing a famous band's songs, and the next you're touring stadiums playing *in* that famous band!) If you're trying to stick to formula, you'll want to bring aboard someone who hews close to the departed team member. But if you think it's time for a new perspective, an approach I'd highly recommend, don't go for the carbon copy.

- *Look outside your comfort zone.* Actively seek the replacement in places you wouldn't normally look. Don't just go with the same corporate headhunter or the same college tours. Change things. Open the door to new faces, new possibilities. In the worst case, you're no worse off than you were before. In the best case, you've totally changed the face of your team and injected new life into your group.
- *Welcome the new ideas from your new face.* Your newcomer will bring along ideas of his or her own. Maybe they'll be terrible, but they're worth considering all the same. You never know when inspiration will strike. If we'd kept Max muzzled and told him to sing only when spoken to, chances are we would have missed out on a smash hit.
- *Just because you've been doing the same thing for so long, that doesn't make it right.* A new voice and a new face can shake up the old way of doing business by bringing a new perspective to the workplace dynamic. Maybe you've fallen into bad habits, or maybe you've worked the same

way for so many years that you don't see the opportunities that are obvious to others. A new voice can help cut through some of the barriers to communication that you might not even know exist, you've lived with them for so long.

Trying to Make It Work

Max ended up doing two records and a tour with us until he decided that the grind of touring wasn't for him. He left the band, and we made overtures to bring Don back into the fold. And for a time, things ran smoothly. But after a few years, as you'd expect, things turned rocky once again.

The difficulties with Don weren't monetary. It was more about power and control. The band wasn't running like a team anymore; it was like a dictatorship. But you can't motivate people through constant negativity. (Now I'll admit there are two sides of this story; Don would surely tell you a different version. But the end result would be the same.)

It was frustrating to have these kinds of differences of opinion keep getting in the way. We'd come a long way from the early days when we were packed into two hotel rooms, having a blast and enjoying every minute of what we were doing. But as we grew more successful, the music became a business, and different members of the team handled that transition in different ways.

It's painful but true: at some point, you may have to cut ties with the team you've been part of for so long. You hope it doesn't happen—plenty of marriages go the distance, plenty of companies survive with their original teams intact—but there are times when it's not worth it to keep going on the way you're going. When you start seeing these signs, it's time to begin thinking of the next chapter in your life:

- *You're not a team any longer.* You started out so closely bonded, everyone on the same page, everyone believing the same things, everyone willing to sacrifice for the greater good of the team. But somewhere along the line, priorities changed. When we were a younger band, we'd expect everyone to be at rehearsal, hell or high water. *Your girlfriend wants to go out on Saturday night? Fine, go—but don't come back on Sunday looking to get back with the band. Make your choice—her or the band.* The further in life you go, though, the more you see beyond the walls of your own world. Maybe after so many years, you want your family to take priority over your work. Or maybe you have a situation where someone's not happy with the politics of a one-person, one-vote team, and he or she wants a larger voice. At that point, you're not a team; you're working in service of one person. And if that's not the direction you want to take, you'll need to think hard about how much longer you want to continue down that path.

- *You've drifted too far from your original mission.* Why did you begin doing what you're doing? Were you driven by a sense of purpose—say, a need to make a difference? A need to save the planet? A need to bring something to people that they hadn't had before? Take a look back at what guided you, what got you started on your path. Are you still on that road, or did you take a detour somewhere along the way? For me, I didn't join a band to argue over songwriting percentages or the nuances of a performance in Des Moines. When that became the focus of my work, I knew that there had to be something else out there for me to pursue.

• *You're outside your comfort zone.* Dan had this problem with a catalogue business he ran selling NASCAR collectibles. It grew so big, so quickly that it was impossible to keep control of it in the way that he wanted. There's a huge difference between the entrepreneurial and the corporate worlds, and when your company moves from the former to the latter, it requires all kinds of new layers of management, infrastructure, and systems. Dan was at a crossroads with his company: he had to take on debt to invest in taking his company to the next level, plus hire a chief operating officer and a new layer of management. Most entrepreneurs are not comfortable letting go of the reins even a little bit. Fortunately for Dan, a different opportunity presented itself; a much larger catalogue company made him an offer he couldn't refuse. It was the right call for him for any number of reasons, and it ended up putting us both in the situation we're in today: a growing company teaching rock 'n' roll and having a blast.

• *You've got other opportunities on the horizon.* The further you go with your team, the more you develop skills that you can take somewhere else if need be. You'll know if there are other opportunities in your own industry, and you can also consider other career lines that might tie in with your own. When I started out playing in a rock band,

I never dreamed I'd be running a rock'n'roll camp (or writing a book, for that matter), and yet here we are! All of this was made possible by my time with 38, but I couldn't have possibly anticipated it would happen back when we were a struggling Jacksonville band. Still, the opportunities presented themselves because I put myself in a position to create and take advantage of them, and you can do the same thing in your own career.

 • *You've outgrown your job.* When you're starting out as a rock band, you've got pretty much one overriding mission: have fun. Playing music, meeting fans, soaking in the roar of the crowd, touring the country: it's all part of that greater goal of just enjoying yourself. But as you get older, responsibilities start crowding in. You start worrying about money and family, and the fun takes a back seat. But you don't have to get rid of the fun entirely. It's possible to be a perfectly mature rock band, as strange as that sounds. Your own career may or may not be as fun as being in a rock band, but you still derived some kind of satisfaction from it beyond just cashing a paycheck. When that satisfaction vanishes, when it's all about the money, it's time to start looking elsewhere.

When I was a kid, I wondered why in the world certain bands would break up. Didn't they understand that they'd never be as successful on their own as they were as a group? Didn't they understand what they'd be doing to their fans by breaking up? Sometimes bands take the patchwork approach—somebody leaves, and they bring in a replacement—but with rare exceptions, the new product doesn't measure up to the original. There's a spark missing, a key piece that helps the entire band function as one seamless unit, and you start to see why the band was on the verge of breaking up. Something's not there any longer.

Bands like U2 and ZZ Top are all the more amazing. These Rock & Roll Hall of Famers have put together careers lasting more than thirty years with the same personnel that they had on day 1. That's not to say there haven't been disagreements within the bands; I'm sure there have been. But these bands have been able to stick together because they've been able to resolve whatever conflicts they have, giving the needs of the band priority over the needs of the individual members. (There's also the case of the Rolling Stones. Although they've had members rotate in and out, they've managed to get past their well-documented personality conflicts, for the simple reason that they're an industry unto themselves. They don't entertain splitting up as even an option.)

It's a matter of give and take. And when one side's doing all the giving and one side's doing all the taking, it's only a matter of time before everything goes south—and not in a good way either.

Verse

There comes a time when a key member has to leave your team, by either his or her choice or yours. Understand when it's time to part ways, and understand

that sometimes there's no salvaging a partnership. Take the separation as an opportunity to look at new directions in your team's development.

Chorus

Consider what the team is losing when a member departs. What elements do you wish to replace, and what elements can be left behind? Is it possible that some existing team members can pick up the slack, or is a replacement absolutely necessary?

Solo

Think about your own limits. Understand what you will and won't put up with from your team. Decide where you're going to compromise and where you're going to stand your ground.

12.

It's the End of the World as We Know It

WHAT TO DO WHEN SOMETHING GOES HORRIBLY WRONG. AND IT WILL. COUNT ON IT.

No matter how many times you prepare and plan for a concert, no matter how many times you rehearse and memorize, something always goes wrong. Perhaps it's something the audience never notices, and perhaps it's something that brings the entire show grinding to a halt. Every performer has a catalogue of horror stories. Here are mine.

The Stage Dive

When we were starting out, we had a rule: one man down, all men down. In other words, if somebody tripped and fell onstage, everybody would hit the deck along with him and start playing to keep the poor guy from getting too embarrassed. Donnie used to flail around all over the stage, so he was usually the one hitting the deck, but it happened to all of us at one time or another. We pulled the all-fall-down trick a few times, and the audience loved it. More important, it kept the whole all-for-one mentality going.

Then one night, I was running across the stage. (The fact that I had room to even walk, much less run, should tell you this was on one of our later tours.) I was going full tilt, and suddenly I realized that my legs weren't keeping up with my upper body. I started falling, and like in a Sam Peckinpah

"Probably the worst gig I can remember was a recording session for the TV show *In the Heat of the Night*. I was part of a band ensemble alongside the Atlanta Symphony Orchestra. It required heavy sight-reading, dozens of scene scores, which I didn't get much call for at the time. So here I am, stopping an entire session cold by taking a wrong turn at a measure, and I've got an entire symphony, guys who can sight-read in their sleep, chuckling at me. I dropped a few pounds that day. . . . A little uncomfortable!"

—GUITARIST PETER STROUD, TEN-YEAR VETERAN OF SHERYL CROW'S BAND movie, everything was happening in slow motion. There was absolutely no way to save this crash, so I pulled my guitar toward me as tight as I could before I hit the stage, and then I went down.

Then we were in real time again. My guitar was squealing a godawful noise, and no matter what I played, it sounded like early, distorted Hendrix. As it turned out, I'd popped out the pickups—the tiny magnets beneath the strings that convert and transmit sound in an electric guitar—and they were resting directly on the strings. Worse, everybody was looking down at me. They'd forgotten the all-for-one routine! I yanked Don Barnes down beside me, then struggled to my feet. My wrist was starting to swell up, and a road guy gave me a spare guitar. I spent the rest of the show with a tender wrist and my backup guitar.

Shoe Fly

This one's more ridiculous than anything else. One night at the Philadelphia Spectrum, I made a kicking motion, only to watch in horror as my shoe went sailing off into the crowd. I could actually see it flying through the spotlight! I figured that was that and kicked off my other shoe to do the show barefoot. I found out later that one of the road crew waded into the audience and got my shoe back. And as a joke of a birthday present, my wife had the shoe bronzed. I have it to this day on a shelf in my den, where it's quite the conversation piece.

Up, Up, and Away

On our second tour, we used a very cool flying rig as part of the climax of our shows. On our last song, Donnie would slip offstage for a moment during a jam and slide into a harness. And on one of the final downbeats, he'd launch off the drum riser and fly up into the arena. He'd go quite a ways out there; in some of the theaters with overhanging balconies, he could get close enough to almost touch the fans in the upper decks.

The flight system worked by using counter-weights—a sandbag just a little heavier than Donnie would lift him into the air. We tested the system every day at sound check before the shows, no matter what. The techs would call "all clear," everyone would get out of the way, and Donnie would fly.

One day in Atlanta, Don Barnes's brother Jim was visiting, so we brought him out to the front of the stage during sound check to watch the testing. Only this time it didn't go so well. Right as the techs dropped the sand-bag, somebody who hadn't been paying attention to the all-clear call walked into the drop zone. If this guy had been hit by the sandbag, he would have been killed, no question. So the techs grabbed the rope and tried to slow the sandbag. But that sent Donnie careening all over the stage, crashing into monitors left and right. He hurt his shoulder so badly that he had to go to the hospital for X-rays.

"That's pretty impressive," Jim said as Donnie banged across the stage, "but you think it's a good idea to do that every night?"

This Way Out

Remember that old bit in *Spinal Tap* where the band runs through the bowels of the arena but can't find the stage? That happens more often than you'd like to believe. Particularly in the Northeast, a lot of the old theaters and arenas have hallways and stairways that don't connect where you think they should. We could hear the audience but wouldn't be able to get anywhere near the stage! So our road manager came up with a good idea: in every arena, he taped fluorescent tape in a line from our dressing room to the stage door. Like Hansel and Gretel following the breadcrumbs, all we had to do was follow the tape.

The Worst of Them All

By far the worst concert I ever experienced—one of the worst concert stories I've ever heard anyone experience—came during our first show with Max. We were in Greenville, South Carolina, and I remember telling some of the newer crew members to expect something to go wrong. It was the first show of a new tour; something always went wrong on the first show, and we'd get through it and laugh about it later.

I had no idea what I was in for.

When the concert began, our other guitarist, Max, and I were standing on risers behind enormous fifty-foot-high scrims of thin fabric. We were backlit, so our five-story-high shadows were projected onto the scrims. We were supposed to play the first few bars of the song, and then the scrims would drop, we'd stride down ramps onto the stage, and the show would begin. We got through the first few bars, and the scrims dropped—but only two of them. Mine stayed up, and there I was, pinned on the riser behind a fifty-foot-high sheet of fabric.

I tried to get the crew's attention, but nobody noticed my problem. So after about twenty seconds, I reached out and grabbed the scrim myself, trying to work my way around it. But the scrim got caught up in my guitar neck, and the Greenville crowd had a vision of a giant wrestling with a piece of cloth.

I later found out why the crew wasn't paying attention to me. It seems Max had wanted to make a big impression in his first live performance as a member of 38 Special, and he certainly did: when he leaped off one riser, he fell face first into his own keyboard. His son, watching from offstage, thought he'd been knocked out cold, but Max got to his feet. So then the show truly began. What else could go wrong?

Plenty.

A few songs later, we were playing "Fantasy Girl," and I sidled up a little too close to Max. He loved doing

James Brown–style microphone-stand baton flips, and he brought the stand right down on the neck of my guitar, taking a huge chunk of wood out from between the fifth and sixth frets and just missing my thumb. I had to switch guitars to finish out the set.

Oh, but we weren't done yet. We were getting toward the end of the show and started playing "Caught Up in You." But Max started singing "I heard you asking . . . "—not the lyrics to "Caught Up in You." Turns out he'd mistaken the song for "Back Where You Belong," another of our songs with a similar guitar-and-drums introduction.

The guys in the band were wide-eyed, and I motioned for everyone to keep playing. Max, beads of sweat running down his forehead, comes over to me and says, "What's the first line?" He'd gone completely blank.

"'I never knew . . . ,'" I replied.

"Thanks for the help," Max shot back sarcastically, much to my confusion.

He scowled at me and headed off elsewhere for help. Turns out he'd misunderstood me—the opening lines of "Caught Up in You" are "I never knew there'd come a day when I'd be saying to you, 'Don't let this good love slip away'"—but Max and I had unwittingly stumbled into an Abbott-and-Costello "Who's on First" routine in the *middle of the song!*

Well, Max owned up to his mistake, and the crowd absolutely loved it, cheering him all the way. After the show, our manager tried to convince us to pull that stunt every show.

No thanks. One nightmare like that was more than enough.

↓↓↓

So what can you do to avert disaster? Nothing. Sad to say, something will always go wrong with your work, and you can only hope it's not in front of twenty thousand people. But even if it is, you can survive it with most of your dignity intact if you keep the right perspective. Mistakes need correction; accidents are often completely unrelated to the competence, skill, or preparation of the team, and are occasionally out of the control of the team entirely.

The best thing about these kinds of mistakes is that they're almost like free passes; they may be someone's fault, but they're so far out of what you'd expect that it's tough to get angry or fault anyone for them. And you can do what I'm able to do: look back and smile. From twenty years' distance, it's a lot easier to laugh.

Verse

Prepare for the worst. You should collaborate as a team to predict any kind of accident or shortcoming that could occur. Bring extra batteries, bring extra copies of presentations, and store important files on the Web where they could be accessed from anywhere with an Internet connection. Think through every eventuality, and try to figure out how to avoid it.

Chorus

Hit the deck with your mates. If someone on your team has a problem, do what you can to cover for him or her. If someone goes blank during a presentation, prompt the person with a question. If the computer malfunctions at a key moment, make arrangements for a replacement. The smoother you're able to cover for your team's problems, the more quickly you'll reach the finish line in (almost) one piece.

Solo

Laugh it off. At some point when everything is going wrong—the computer is blown, the mike won't work, and you can't remember the next line of your presentation—give it up and laugh. If the fates are stacked against you, getting angry or upset only encourages them.

13

Should I Stay or Should I Go?

HOW TO KNOW WHEN IT'S TIME TO MOVE ON, AND HOW TO DEVELOP AN EXIT STRATEGY BEFORE YOU DO.

In 1991, we were riding high, still basking in the glow of our best-selling song. We were in a comfortable songwriting partnership, and even with a new lead singer, we had a well-defined sound. Like Journey and Foreigner, we were a brand name, known all over the country. It was a very good time to be a veteran rock star.

And then three scruffy kids from Seattle came and pulled the rug right out from under all of us.

That same year Nirvana released "Nevermind," officially kicking off the grunge era in rock music. Grunge was a conscious rejection of the attitude that had grown up around rock, if not the style of music itself. (Nirvana's groundbreaking hit, "Smells Like Teen Spirit," is based on a riff that's almost identical to Boston's "More Than a Feeling.") Suddenly soaring choruses and screaming guitar solos were out; raw distortion and confessional lyrics were in. And it literally happened that fast. "Nevermind" instantly rendered a hundred platinum-selling hair-metal bands obsolete. Those bands, which specialized in flashy outfits, explosive stage shows, and hard-partying attitudes, have never recovered even a fraction of the audience they had the day before "Nevermind" hit the stands, and they never will. Tastes change—sometimes gradually and sometimes, as in the Nirvana example, instantly.

Over the course of the fifteen years since we'd started, record companies had transformed from places that nurtured artists, giving them three albums to prove themselves, as A&M did with us, to flavor-of-the-month warehouses, where each record company wanted whatever was popular at that very moment, and nothing else. Chasing trends among the record companies was nothing new; it's what got us signed when we were brand new and everyone wanted some Southern rock in their stable. But over the years, the time had become compressed; bands went from having years to prove themselves to having months (and, now, weeks).

So when the record companies saw that this little Seattle band had struck a raggedy, distorted chord with its audience, they sent fleets of jets up to Seattle to sign anything that even resembled a grunge band. Although a few good bands got picked up in that feeding frenzy— Pearl Jam is still making good records to this day, for instance—there were a lot of very disposable bands that got signed because they wore flannel and had bad haircuts.

Needless to say, this made bands like Journey, Foreigner, Bon Jovi, and us instantly out-of-date. What record company wanted a bunch of expensive guys in their late thirties and early forties playing guitar when they could sign and promote a bunch of young, hot bands at a fraction of the cost, and with more control over what the band put out? For the record companies, it was a no-brainer. And although huge chunks of the public still enjoyed what we were doing, the segment with the most disposable income, younger fans, was looking in directions other than ours.

Of all the bands from that era, Bon Jovi far and away fared the best. And they did it with some masterful moves. They spent most of the 1990s in Europe and Asia, places where, for whatever reason, grunge didn't have nearly the same kind of genre-crushing impact that it had over here. And while they were over there entertaining enormous crowds with "Wanted: Dead or Alive," they were reinventing themselves as an adult pop-country band. So by the time they returned to America around 2000, grunge had played itself out and the band's old fans were ready to hear some new music. Bon Jovi found itself not only accepted but welcomed, and it became a bigger band than ever before. It was an extremely methodical approach, and one that other bands would have done well to imitate.

We didn't. The rest of us weren't nearly that savvy. Everybody else fought the rising tide of grunge, using the same kinds of phrases that our parents had used when talking about Elvis Presley: *That music stinks! That kid needs to clean himself up! This'll never last!*

Bad Signs All Around

And then we started noticing some disturbing things. For instance, record companies started asking for demos—rough-draft versions of songs—before we'd enter the studio. The bands, naturally enough, went ballistic. *Demos? Are you serious?* In 38, we never sent demos of new material. We would even pick which record guys got to come into our studio; there were certain executives we didn't want anywhere near us when we were making records.

So we fought the demo requests. But then came the style requests. The record labels started giving us advice on how to create our records. *You're doing a new record? Great! Is it going to sound like the old stuff? We LOVE that!* The problem with that is that the old stuff isn't going to get played on the radio, so you have to be somewhat open-minded to what's going on around you.

But on the other side of that equation, we had to be at least somewhat true to our roots. We weren't going to become a grunge band: we wouldn't know how to do it, it wouldn't be honest, and our fans would revolt.

We were between a rock and a hard place, and we weren't alone in that arena.

The next red flag—and this was a huge one that nobody missed—was that the old record companies stopped re-signing the old bands. Suddenly, when your contract ran out, you weren't necessarily guaranteed of hooking up again with your record company for a three-album deal. You'd have to start shopping for independent record companies, places with names you'd never heard of, with weak distribution deals that didn't always make it easy for your customer to find your product.

And the touring landscape changed dramatically as well. The first time we were asked to play a state fair, we were stunned at the idea. *Really? A state fair?* We'd been playing *stadiums*, for heaven's sake. A state fair seemed a steep drop in prestige.

No, our tour managers assured us, *it's not like that. This is the Ohio State Fair. It's huge; you're going to love it.* And you know what? They were right. It was a huge gig with twenty-five thousand people. We ate well, we had a good time, and we really enjoyed ourselves. We decided we could get used to the state fair circuit.

But the next time, we weren't getting booked at state fairs. We were getting booked at *county* fairs. And then we were back to playing clubs again after all this time. And we started asking, "Any more of those county fairs available?"

At some point, you have to acknowledge that you're on the back side of the curve and going the opposite way from success. Very few bands are able to pick up the pieces from that point and make another run of it.

We had to understand that we were in a new reality in the music industry and that everything that had gotten us here no longer applied. We had to weigh our options; a bunch of us had made a living at this for twenty-five years. Did we want to try to make it for thirty-five or forty-five?

We had to ask ourselves whether, in this new climate, we thought we'd be able to achieve the levels of success we'd had before. And all the signs seemed to indicate that we wouldn't. At this point, each band has to make a decision: keep on doing what they've been doing, hoping things will turn around, or make a conscious choice to take a different path.

Some bands, whether because they got stubborn or lazy, didn't change their approach at all. They assumed that they could just keep on doing what had worked well for them, completely ignoring the new reality. You don't hear much from those bands anymore.

Others have tried to repackage their past for new consumption, trading on nostalgia and past glories. They package tours, joining forces with other famous names and banding together for what are, in effect, greatest-hits tours. They don't even need to release new material; they just play their back catalogue over and over again.

I had two realizations, both of which pushed me toward a difficult decision. First, I realized that in the early 1990s, it was the beginning of the end: the way it was then was the way it was going to be for a long time to come. I had to be honest with myself that the chances of getting back on top were slim indeed. Did I really want to keep playing my old hits, year after year, in front of the same crowds that were growing older along with me? What was the future in that?

Second, I could see the impact that this changing environment was having on us as a band. Frustrations, tensions, and a lack of hope were all building up. Nobody was happy with the direction that things were going, and since you can't blame all your problems on a fickle public or Kurt Cobain, you start blaming each other.

"It would be great if you could sit down with your band before you play your first gig and say, 'This is how we're going to divide it out; I'm going to be the star and get this much, and you guys are going to be my band and get this much.' When you're playing high schools and parties, laying that groundwork never occurs to you. But it's the kind of thing that should be done as soon as you can. There will be problems and arguments, but it's better when they're small."

—LIBERTY DEVITTO, CAMP JAM MASTER CLASS DRUMMER AND THIRTY-YEAR VETERAN OF BILLY JOEL'S BAND

We had come a long way from the kids we were in Jacksonville. Our original lineup had gotten diluted as guys came and went, and the family was fracturing. There were now guys I didn't like in the band, and there were guys who didn't like me. The band environment was getting more cutthroat by the day; people were talking behind each other's back, and the atmosphere had turned poisonous.

The band was on a downward slope. My occupation had gone from the best thing in the world, living out a dream and traveling the world, to the point that I didn't even want to go to work anymore. Key personalities were constantly fighting; we were like oil and water, and we could see that there was no getting around the fact that we didn't get along.

Calling It a Day

By 1994, it was clear to me that things weren't going to get any better. I had interests outside the band, and I started realizing it was time to look into them. It was time to move on. We reached a mutual decision that it was time for me to call it a day with 38 and move on to the next phase of my life. The last album I played on was 1991's *Bone Against Steel,* and although some of my songs ended up on 1997's *Resolution,* I wasn't involved with the making of that album at all.

It's a lot easier to reinvent yourself as an individual than it is as a band. On your own, you can open yourself up to new influences and new ways of looking at music. So that was what I wanted to try, to see what else I still had in the tank.

It wasn't so difficult making the break with 38; by that time, so much water had passed under the bridge since Jacksonville that it would have felt wrong to stay. But by the same token, this band was an enormous part of my life, and so cutting loose from it put a lot of stress on me, even though I knew it was the right thing to do.

There will come a time when your own industry will bear little resemblance to the time you entered it or the way it is now. And that's terrifying: everything you've taken for granted suddenly no longer exists. I've been there. You don't want to live your life expecting doomsday to arrive, but you also don't want to get caught by surprise when it does come around. Nirvana caught every single one of us flatfooted, but as Bon Jovi showed, we still had enough time to weather the storm if we'd made the right choices. With a little forethought, you can prepare for the worst:

• *Accept that the good times will end.* It's going to happen, like it or not. Nothing good lasts forever. Customers' tastes change; the economy rises and falls. You don't want to be the person at the party predicting doom-and-gloom in the midst of boom times, but you also don't want to be the one left cleaning up after the party. Too many of my peers simply assumed that grunge was a fad, not a completely new movement in music, and they were astonished to find out that they had been utterly replaced in both the public eye and on store shelves.

• *Pay attention to the cultural landscape.* The Internet gives everyone a chance to take the pulse of the cultural landscape in a way that would have been unimaginable even fifteen years ago. If the Internet had been around in its current form in 1991, savvy music fans would have spotted Nirvana coming from a mile away. That grassroots groundswell is important to keep in mind; the major tastemakers in any field can control the marketplace for only so long before a new trend breaks through. And if you're on the wrong side of that trend—as we were in 1991, as network television and newspapers seem to be now—you'd better do everything you can to get yourself ready for the high tide. For instance, if you've staked your entire future on green products and survey after survey shows that people aren't as concerned about the environment as they say they are, it might be time to rethink your business strategy.

• *Observe the newcomers to your field.* Always keep an eye on your competition, and in particular, watch the newest entrants to your competitive space. What do they have that hasn't been offered before? How are people responding to it? Also, here's an uncomfortable question that you need to respond to: If you were coming into this field right now, with what you're offering right now, how well would you do without the name recognition you've built up? If you can't honestly say you'd dominate the space to the same degree you do now, it's time to start thinking up some new strategic alternatives.

• *Start implementing your exit strategy.* Nobody plans to be robbed, but we have security systems anyway. Nobody plans to have their house catch fire, but we keep insurance anyway. And yet so many people just assume their careers—or, thinking larger, their entire industry— will keep humming along merrily until they decide it's time to get off the train and do something else. But it doesn't work that way. You've got to have a plan in place to handle the bottom falling out. Maybe that's a full-scale strategy for diversifying into other lines of business; maybe it's as simple as keeping a few months' salary on ice and maintaining your contacts across industry lines. Whatever you do, remember that it's better to have such a plan and never need it than suddenly need it and never have made one.

Verse

Times change, and tastes change with them. You've got to accept that fact going into any endeavor. That doesn't mean that your own particular operation or team comes with an expiration date, but your way of doing business, your way of appealing to the public, certainly does. Changes, even seismic ones, can occur instantly, so do everything you can to prepare for them.

Chorus

When change hits, you've got to decide how to react. But by then, it's already too late to be coming up with strategies. You need to prepare as a team for the eventuality of change, for the possibility that what's worked for so long isn't going to work any longer. Take the time to weigh alternatives and consider options long before you've got the proverbial gun to your head.

Solo

Observe the reasons behind certain companies' or industries' failure—the way that they were unable to adapt to change. Think about what you can learn from a band that didn't keep up with popular tastes or an industry that underestimated the power of the Internet. Then see if you can apply those lessons to your own company.

No Particular Place to Go

SO YOU'VE LEFT YOUR OLD LIFE, THE ONE YOU'VE KNOWN FOR DECADES. WHAT DEFINES YOU NOW? AND HOW LONG ARE YOU GOING TO KEEP HANGING AROUND THE HOUSE?

hat first day out of the band, I couldn't stop thinking that what I'd known all my adult life was gone. All I could focus on was what I'd lost. Those first few months when I was at home without a place to go, an album to record, or a song to write, I wasn't quite sure what to do with myself. Certainly it was great fun being with my family, particularly my young daughter. But I'd spent more than two decades in the write-record-tour cycle, so I was at a loss for how to live a different life.

At the heart of the problem was the fact that I didn't know how to define myself any longer. I was now a former member of 38 Special: that much was certain. But was I still a guitarist, or was I an ex-guitarist? Could I use my musical background in other areas, or should I start up another band? I started dabbling in various—well, let's call them "professional hobbies." I was throwing out line after line, seeing if something bit.

One of my early post-38 endeavors was something that sprang out of an event that we did back in 1994. Al Unser Jr., the racecar driver, had won the Indy 500 that year, and he was having a charity bash in Albuquerque. His wife was apparently a huge 38 Special fan, so he gave us a call and wanted us to play at the event.

I looked at our itinerary and saw that we were on tour then, and it almost broke my heart. We had to be in Mobile, Alabama, the night after Little Al's show. I called him back and said, "I'm sorry, Al, but we're not going to be able to do it. There's no way we'll be able to get our equipment back to Mobile in time for the show that night." I'm a huge race fan, and I knew a bunch of my favorite drivers were going to be there, so this was killing me that I couldn't take part in this.

And then Al made everything work: "Tell us what equipment you need. We'll get it for you. Send your truck on to Mobile." Then he sent a Gulfstream jet to fly us to New Mexico and back. (Once you've flown in a Gulfstream, every other kind of transportation is second-rate. We landed in Mobile after Al's event, and our tour bus was waiting for us on the tarmac. We'd loved that tour bus, but getting on that after being in a Gulfstream just plunged us into depression.)

For the event, I decided to present Al with a special souvenir: a guitar decorated with his number and sponsors. A guy named Wayne Jarrett in Greensboro, North Carolina, made the guitar for us, and it was an instant hit. Every driver, every executive at this charity event wanted one custom-made. So we started doing a little toe-dip into the world of custom guitars.

This was around the time that I was leaving 38, and I was looking for another activity to occupy my time. This combined racing and music, two of my passions, and so I was excited about the idea. A contact of mine at ESPN, whom I'd known since 38, when I did some of the music for ESPN's NASCAR telecasts, told me how hot NASCAR collectibles were getting, and recommended I see about putting these custom guitars in the NASCAR catalogue. He introduced me to Dan Lipson, who ran the catalogue and "Shop Talk," the NASCAR collectibles show on ESPN. Dan, who, as it turned out, lived about a mile away from me in Atlanta, helped me negotiate the maze of licensing that goes with anything done with NASCAR.

We negotiated agreements with Rusty Wallace and Jeff Gordon, and their guitars were both big sellers— quite a feat considering they cost twenty-five hundred dollars apiece. A deal to get the license of the late, great Dale Earnhardt fell apart at the last second.

Soon after, though, Dan sold the NASCAR catalogue company, and the new owners had a bad habit of

"Once you've achieved a certain level of success, you tend to keep moving forward. It's a powerful motivator to explore other areas, including those unforeseen opportunities you never thought about. I've learned through the years to keep a wide field of vision. In the past, every time a tour would draw to close I'd be concerned . . . usually about money! But I found when I'd stop worrying, an unexpected opportunity would always present itself. In the past, I'd never admit to my cover band days. But later, because of those years, I can play or at least assimilate most any style. It's proven very valuable—an ability I wouldn't have had, had I limited myself."

—GUITARIST PETER STROUD, TEN-YEAR VETERAN OF SHERYL CROW'S BAND

not paying in a particularly timely manner. I realized that I needed to start looking elsewhere when I caught myself waking up at night worrying about what was supposed to be a diversion and a hobby. I closed up shop but left the business having made a contact in Dan, who would change the direction of my life a few years later.

Although I wasn't in a band any longer, I never lost the desire to keep playing music. I'd just grown tired of all the politics and offstage problems that surrounded playing in 38. Around the time that the NASCAR guitars gig fell apart, I started making phone calls and seeing who was available to play a gig or two. Drummer Michael Cartellone and I convinced vocalist Derek St. Holmes from Ted Nugent's band, guitarist Pat Travers, and bass player Benjamin Orr of the Cars to get together and see what happened. Michael got an invitation to join a new version of Skynyrd, so Liberty DeVitto of Billy Joel's band decided to jump aboard.

All of a sudden, I was like the retired CEO who gets involved in a tiny start-up. I was back in my Jacksonville days, kicking around with a new band—the most phenomenally talented band I'd ever had the pleasure to play with. When told of the roster, one of Pat's friends said, "Wow, that's some big people!" It was the perfect name for our new band.

We were all veterans of the music business and took a lot of pleasure in opening up each of our closets and comparing skeletons. But we also worked ourselves up to professional grade, even winning a slot opening up for Styx. We'd play songs from each of our old bands, reveling in our history and looking forward to the future. It was a bit of a change, going back to being an opening act after so many years as a headliner, but I was long past worrying about those kinds of things. I didn't see it as something to be embarrassed about; I was playing music with good friends and enjoying the rock life again, so what could possibly be the problem?

But Big People never got the momentum we hoped; in May 2000, Ben learned that he had pancreatic cancer, and in October he passed away. That was devastating to us, and while we haven't ever officially disbanded Big People, we never did get around to recording a CD. Both Derek and Liberty are now good friends, as well as in-demand counselors and regular "master class" teachers at our Camp Jam events.

Still, Big People opened doors for us. A few years back, the Rock & Roll Hall of Fame invited Liberty, me, and several other musicians to serve as judges for the Battle of the Corporate Bands, an event where employees from companies join together to create their own bands. The interesting thing to me was watching an executive playing side-by-side with some guy from the loading docks, both of them getting off on the whole musical vibe.

"You can't let yourself get stuck doing just one thing. I play music, but I've also written drum instruction books, and I make as much, if not more, off those than my music. When you're going from the stage to the clinic, it recharges you, and you can bring your best effort to both of them."
—CARMINE APPICE, DRUMMER FOR OZZY OSBOURNE AND ROD STEWART

We got along so well with the Hall of Fame people that they invited us to serve as the house band for their annual gala. We back up musical legends past and present, and it's an unbelievable trip to see some of our heroes from our youth sharing a stage right there with us. We played with Paul Shaffer and Will Lee of David Letterman's band, backing people like Ronnie Spector, Mitch Ryder, Patty Smythe, and many others. They raised the bar for me and forced me to bring my "A" game in a way I hadn't for years.

More important, Big People convinced me that I still had the music itch, but that a whole new band might not be the best way to scratch it. In 2003, Dan and I began kicking around the idea of a rock 'n' roll camp for adults. There were already a couple such camps in existence, so we decided, much as we had in 38 years before, not to copy what others were already doing. Dan had already launched another successful company, Leading Edge

Promotions, which worked with tennis, golf, and bowling organizations to create programs that exponentially increased youth participation. The answer was obvious: it was time to take rock to kids.

In 2004, we launched the first camp in Atlanta, and it was a big success. We took it to Houston and Dallas the next year, and then branched out across the country. We now have sixteen camps, including one in Canada, each taking a hundred kids for a week and honing them into budding rock stars. The adult camp came to life in its own way as a corporate training event.

But it was the kids' camp that got us our first national attention, thanks to some fortunate media coverage. The *Atlanta Journal-Constitution* ran an article on us, and it happened to catch the attention of a *Los Angeles Times* reporter who was in town. (Connections, circumstance, coincidence: you never know how these things will play out.) The reporter hung out for a week, then called ten days later to let us know that we were on the front page—and not the front page of the Life section, the front page of the paper. That day, it was Bush, Iraq, Camp Jam.

By the time the West Coast woke up and saw the headline, our phone began ringing. *NBC Nightly News, The Today Show, Time* Magazine, *People,* CNN: suddenly everyone wanted a piece of us. Dan and I started taking meetings with reality show producers, but those meetings went nowhere. Almost all the producers wanted to set Camp Jam up as a competition, with one kid winning and another losing and, hopefully, crying on camera. That wasn't what we were all about, so we politely declined that option and stuck with what we had: an environment where all the kids enjoy themselves, and there are no losers.

Today Camp Jam is expanding faster than we'd ever imagined possible. In just a few years, we've gone from an idea to a nationwide phenomenon. We're now active in twenty markets, and we've taught tens of thousands of young students how to rock. We've developed a line of music books, the adult rock camp, an MTV show, and an interactive social network site, jamling.com, which allows young musicians to form virtual bands. Musicians can download the elements of their favorite songs and insert their own work—playing bass on "I Love Rock 'n' Roll," say—and then post their versions for others to hear. It's the twenty-first-century equivalent of my Jacksonville high school days, except now we have an entire country of possible bandmates.

Having a solid company is a tremendous reward, but knowing we're changing lives in a positive way makes it all worthwhile. I never expected to be here at this point in my life, but now that I am, I couldn't be happier.

Verse

Your work is a large chunk of your identity. And when it goes, a large chunk of your self goes with it. There's no way to prevent that, but you can start searching around to make connections between what you've done before and what you could be doing next. Eventually something will click for you, and when it does, you'll find it every bit as rewarding as your previous career.

Chorus

As a team, brainstorm the possibilities beyond your career now. It's almost heresy, and you probably don't want to be doing it on company time, but think about how the skills you've developed can translate into other worlds. After all, you probably won't lose contact with all of your team after your time with them is done. Why not start setting up that contact network right now?

Solo

Imagine yourself without your current job; imagine no jobs in your current field are even available to you. What will you do next? How will you move your career forward? It's a scary thought; and I hope it will remain a hypothetical.

Second Chance

can a rock 'n' roller survive in a corporate world?

I can look back on my years in 38 with pride. We made some great music, and some that I truly believe will stand the test of time. And we're now at that twenty-year point where people start rediscovering our music; a lot of us songwriters are noticing an uptick in royalties in some songs as they start showing up in movies and video games. Guitar Hero has done a world of good for us, helping a whole new generation of fans discover our music.

The further that we get from the 1970s and 1980s, the more we see that the music that came out of that era is going to last a lot longer and be a lot more memorable than most of the flavor-of-the-month music. We'll keep hearing these songs again and again on classic rock radio and in movies and commercials, because to my mind there's an authenticity there that's sorely lacking when you're just trying to follow a trend.

The bands that lived through that era are still trying to break some new ground, if not in the expected ways. Bands like Journey will probably never have a major radio hit again, but they've continued to play off their own history; not too long ago they re-recorded all their hits with their new singer, who sounds exactly like the legendary Steve Perry. Whether that's the right or wrong thing to do with their history is up to the listener, but you have to give the band credit for not standing still.

As for 38? As I write this, there are now two original members left in the band. They continue to tour, playing clubs and fairs around the country, and there are fans who are still dedicated to the band. Knowing what I know now, I can see that I made the right decision for me. Had I stayed with the band, I would have missed out not only on all the family experiences I had, but also on the opportunity to build a new business with Dan. It's important to me to always be ready to accept challenges. If you allow yourself to get stagnant, you'll lose any drive you had to get better.

I also got lucky to get out of the music business when I did. Music is one of the most difficult, unfair businesses in the world, particularly with the new technology that's reshaped the industry. I'm glad I'm not a part of it. I'm starting to get a grasp on how new bands define their business model, and it's completely different from the way that we did business.

Kids These Days

Songwriters today don't make much money because so much music is illegally downloaded or given away for free. So no musician can expect a huge profit off one or two hit songs. But these young artists are smart; they've figured out a way to use their songs as a vehicle for self-promotion. They're not just selling a song; they're selling a whole experience, and the song is the gateway. So they'll give a song or two, or even a whole album, away for free, letting people stream it from their Web site or download it to their iPods. I couldn't have imagined doing that in our day, but these young artists realize they can make money on the back end. They can repackage the music into ring tones or sell it to advertisers for commercials. They can turn a tidy profit on merchandise or touring, which is why ticket prices have taken off in the last few years.

Bands today have a tougher road than ever before to reach financial success, but ironically, the Internet has given them an easier road than ever before to public access. Anybody with an acoustic guitar and a microphone can have an MP3 up on the Web and ready for worldwide download in minutes. That's power and access to the fans that we would have killed for when we were starting out.

I don't completely understand the twists and turns the music industry has taken since I left, but I do know enough to realize that I'm out of the loop. I enjoyed it while I was there, but now I'm happy to leave those headaches to others.

From Band to Boardroom

Rarely do I look back at my history with any sort of nostalgia or longing. I don't find a whole lot of value in doing that unless I'm learning from a mistake. But while I do value the time I spent in 38, leaving it behind provided me with opportunities beyond what I could have achieved in the band. I never would have gotten to meet the guys in Big People, who have since become some of my closest friends. I never would have gotten to play with some of my heroes as part of the house band at the Rock & Roll Hall of Fame. And I never would have been able to pass on my love of music to the next generation.

But I wouldn't have gotten involved in the corporate world, which has its own set of drawbacks. For instance, I can't stand e-mail. I know I'm going to sound like a cranky old guy for saying that, but e-mail and voice mail drive me nuts.

Let me explain in a little more detail. I'm involved with the new "band" now: my team that makes up Camp

Jam Inc. Our rock 'n' roll camps for both kids and corporations give everybody a chance to see what it's like to be a rock star for a day or a week. It's a thrill for anyone who straps on a guitar, and it's a great way for me to remain connected to the music business, passing on some traditions and lessons from my days onstage to kids who are just starting out and grown-ups in the corporate world who thought their rock star dreams were long dead. It's something I couldn't have possibly anticipated when I was with 38, but it's been a perfect fit.

Well, almost perfect. The transition from the rock 'n' roll lifestyle to the business environment was pretty jarring, as you can imagine. When I left rock 'n' roll behind, I didn't have any idea what I was getting myself into. Learning the ways of the business world has been like learning a new language for me. Sometimes I slip into my old habits, and sometimes that's not necessarily a bad thing.

But it wasn't that I really missed the rock life. For every crowd that's screaming your name, you've got hours of travel and time away from your family. And remember how I said being in a band is like being married to five other people? Keeping a "marriage" going among six people can be a lot trickier than with just a single partner. There is plenty in the rock world that I don't miss at all.

But there are parts of the business world that don't suit me, and that's where I can bring in a little rock perspective. There are ways that people in the corporate world behave that are so foreign to me that I can't even begin to understand them. And while my way may ruffle a few feathers, it's worked well enough for me so far.

A case in point is communication. As far as I'm concerned, you can't devote enough time to focusing on communication among your team. It's the only way to get anything done, the only way to make sure you're all on the same path. You're communicating with your bandmates every instant that you're onstage, and not just verbally. You watch what they're playing, you listen for their tempo, you feel their time signatures, and you pay attention to every element of what goes on around you.

That doesn't always work in the business world. In fact, every day we move further away from that kind of physical, face-to-face contact. It's a funny thing about communication: as it gets faster and as there are more and more ways to communicate with one another, we're actually communicating much less effectively.

Don't get me wrong: e-mail has its merits. It has made everybody's lives easier and keeps people in contact with one another. But it lacks the human touch of a phone call.

In 2008, a guy I'd worked with on a Camp Jam project told me about a term that he and his team employed in regard to e-mail: *the handoff.* The handoff comes about when you put everything you need to in your e-mail, send it off to someone else, and then wipe your hands of it. *It's your problem now! Call me when you've fixed it!* With the handoff, the assumption is that it's taken care of—always a dangerous assumption to make.

Back in the days of 38, we didn't have the option of e-mailing or texting our manager or our record company, and even if we had, I wouldn't have wanted to. If we had a problem or a question, we'd pick up the phone and get in somebody's face if we needed to.

But that's what we knew as musicians. When you're in a band and going onstage, you don't pull your punches. You don't live your life in moderation. You shoot from the hip. There's no alternative: if you don't say exactly what you mean when you mean it, the world's moving too fast for you to catch up and make changes later.

> "Follow-through is important. I used to write lots of letters to people, and still do sometimes, but of course e-mail has taken over a lot of that. However, letters still have a strong impact and are so much more personal. It does take time and effort, and certainly isn't as convenient as writing an e-mail, but it can have more of an impact if you are really wanting to get to know a person."
>
> —CHUCK LEAVELL, KEYBOARD PLAYER FOR ERIC CLAPTON AND THE ROLLING STONES

Does it lead to hurt feelings? Absolutely. But in the long run, a few hurt feelings are a small price to pay for direct, honest communication. Some people think of it as an intimidation factor; I think of it more as a way to get your point across in the most direct way possible. People may not like it at first, but they respect it, and they learn how to work within your framework.

Let me draw on a specific example. Our Camp Jam Inc. corporate events are always a huge hit with both companies and employees because they give people a chance to become rock stars. That's the key connection there—the connection between us, the new players, and their instruments.

But that's not the only connection we have to make when we're planning these events. We have to go through a number of different bureaucracies, from event planners to equipment manufacturers, and each one of them has a certain way of thinking that's almost alien to me. They work by voice mail and e-mail, and it can be nearly impossible to get a person on the phone. And once you do, it can be extremely difficult to get that person to see beyond what he or she is accustomed to. Although we're a business, we're not a button-down one, and that can confuse some inflexible people.

At our engagements, we generally get about four hours with our new musicians, which is enough time to get them introduced to our philosophy and whip them into serviceable musical shape. (If you can count to four, you can play with us. No kidding.) It can be a terrifying experience for someone who's never played an instrument before—*hey, how are you, here's your guitar, you're going to be onstage in three hours*—so we do our best to put everyone at ease.

One of the easiest ways to do that is by an icebreaker social the night before. We like to hook up with the company at a cocktail party or dinner, introduce ourselves, and then get the ball rolling. There's the initial awe—*Real rock stars! Here!*—but that goes away pretty quickly once everyone realizes we're just regular guys. Everyone wants to hear the stories: *What's it like going onstage? Ever meet a groupie?* And we do a little bonding right there over drinks.

Although the social hour isn't what we're there for, it's value for everybody: the employees enjoy some good stories, and we get everyone prepped for what we're all about, so they have a better idea of what they're walking into the next morning. In addition, they've seen us, they know us, and they're more at ease. Communication has been established, and now the learning can begin.

Some corporate types, though, don't get the value of this kind of bonding. They can't see past scheduling, and if we're scheduled to run our Camp Jam event on one day, there's no reason for us to be a part of the schedule the day before. Some have gone so far as to say they want our appearance to be a "surprise"; they want to keep it secret from their employees until the last minute. I don't know about you, but if I weren't a musician, I couldn't imagine anything more terrifying than walking into a room, seeing a whole bunch of guitars and drums, and being told I was going onstage in front of my peers and bosses in just a few hours.

Most often, the problem is the go-betweens—the people who aren't actually making decisions but are carrying out others' decisions. We've had so many cases where we knew we could resolve problems if we could only talk to a decision maker. That's the nature of business today, and I understand it, but I don't have to like it. I prefer another method, one we can call:

How to Communicate Like a Rock Star

- *Everything's better live.* Which is the better way to experience your favorite music: sitting at home listening on iPod headphones, or sitting front row at a concert with your heroes right there in front of you? Exactly. Everything is better when it's in person, and that goes doubly so for communications. Don't send an e-mail or text when you can make a call. Don't make a call when you can have a face-to-face visit. Yes, everyone's busy, and technology increases efficiency. But efficiency and productivity aren't always the same thing. We could have put out seven albums a year if we weren't interested in quality, but we took the time to do our music right and make a connection with the listener. Similarly, if you take a bit more time to get your message across in person, it'll save dozens of those dreaded "RE: FW:" e-mail trees.

• *Say what you mean.* Your mother had it right: honesty is the best policy. If there's a problem or a question, say so. No more "running it up the flagpole" or "blue-skying" or "building consensus." Business has invented dozens of jargony phrases to avoid saying anything specific, and my question is, Why? Why not get to the heart of the issue from the start? I'm not saying to bulldog your way into conversations or avoid small talk, but think of it in terms of a concert. When those lights go down, the band doesn't come out and start talking to you about your drive over or the ball game, do they? Heck, no: they're right into it from the first chord. There's no mistaking why they're there, no misunderstanding their message.

• *No handoffs. Ever.* When you're onstage, in the heat of a concert, you're engaged every moment of every song. You can't step up, deliver your solo, and then say, "Okay, I'm outta here. You guys run with it." Every member of the team is right there plugged in. Even if they're not playing or singing, they're keeping time and waiting for the right moment to jump back in. Certainly you have to wait for your teammates to deliver on their end of the task at hand, but within reason. Don't simply assume a task is done just because it's out of your in-box.

- *Every once in awhile, smash something.* This one's fun in theory but a bit dicey in practice. Still, every so often, somebody falls so far short of what they need to be doing that you need to bring a little heat. Smash a guitar, so to speak. Use sparingly. Pyrotechnics optional.

Now these techniques aren't for everyone. Some people prefer the calm, moderate hum of corporate communication to the in-your-face rock 'n' roll style. And if it works for them, it's fine. But I've seen too many companies that have huge flaws in their communication structure, and the companies aren't even aware of their problems. It's like trying to carry water with a teaspoon: no matter how careful you are, the more times you pass information around before it reaches its recipient, you're going to lose a good chunk of it along the way.

And I'll freely admit that the rock life isn't always the best life. Your work is always with you, particularly on tour. The team you're with on the road is your family— you form a bond with them that, in many cases, is closer than your own family. And that can cause plenty of stress at home, without a doubt. In the earliest days of 38, we expected everybody to put the band first, before friends, family, or girlfriends. The further that we went along, the more stress the band placed on family relationships. It's tough keeping a marriage together when you're in a rock band, tough keeping together any kind of relationship outside the band framework.

But within the band, within the team, you can bond as a unit. We allocated our responsibilities based on our own skills. Each guy had his own responsibilities and his role, and we all had faith that the other guy would carry out his side of the deal to the best of his ability.

Not everyone could do every job, and not everyone was necessary for every job. We initially did radio interviews with all of us in the studio, and when the DJ asked us a question, you'd hear six voices trying to answer at once. So we divided up the responsibilities, keeping the more outgoing guys up front and the quieter ones focused on other tasks. I was one of the spokesmen and songwriters; other guys kept an eye on tour planning or studio time or publicity or any of a hundred other things that can consume a band's time.

Still, even with a divided set of responsibilities, the band life can be wearing. You shouldn't take your job home with you, yet that's exactly what you end up doing. You're either living on the road, or you're home thinking about your next move. It's a rush, connecting so deeply with your team that you can't imagine doing anything else, but it's also a limited engagement. At some point, you realize you've outgrown the team or the team has moved beyond you, and it's time to turn your eyes in another direction.

I'm in more of a nine-to-five job now, with the exception of our corporate events and summer camps, but it's still a band in a way. I've got my partner, Dan

Lipson, and several other people involved in Camp Jam. It's a great group of people—a cohesive unit where everyone has their own responsibilities and their own roles, and it's a creative environment where we can throw a lot of fun ideas back and forth.

I'd like to think that's at least in part because of my experience with 38, learning to bridge the gap between the creative and the corporate worlds. Back then, I'd walk on the stage, and the crowd would literally be at my feet. You can't *not* enjoy that feeling; it's a rush unlike anything else in the world. And if you're smart, you'll do what you can to protect what's gotten you to that point.

But we tried not to get sucked into believing that it would last forever, because it didn't—not at that level, at least. Some of my old bandmates are still touring, doing festivals and fairs, and I wish them the best. For me, I'm more than happy to spend my time playing a few outings a year, playing in the Rock & Roll Hall of Fame house band, and bringing kids and grown-ups alike through Camp Jam. It's a good gig.

And hearing my own songs on the radio never gets old. To this day, I'll be driving and I'll turn on XM's Top Tracks or the local classic rock station, and "Second Chance" or "Rockin' into the Night" will come on, and for a moment I'm right back there in the middle of everything. I'm listening to my own playing and scrutinizing the sound, and I never get tired of hearing those songs.

My daughter was hanging out with a friend recently when the friend handed over her iPod headphones and said, "I just got this cool new song. You've got to hear this."

It was "Hold on Loosely." No kidding.

My daughter wasn't sure if this was a joke or something, but her friend was stunned to learn that this was *her dad* playing that song. And over the past few years, my daughter has started to realize that her dad—the guy who was always just "Dad" to her—was actually into something pretty cool back before she was born. Her teachers tell her about seeing me in concert back in their high school days and ask if they can get something autographed. It's a lot of fun for both of us (me probably more than her).

It all came together one night not too long ago. Bon Jovi was in town, and I took my daughter to the sound check before the show. As we were walking in, the road crew—many of whom used to work for us back in the old days—came up and embraced me. And when Jon Bon Jovi and the rest of the band came out onstage and welcomed me, my daughter couldn't believe it. I tried to tell her, "These guys used to *open* for me back in 1986!"

Still, it wasn't until the show began that everything clicked for my daughter. We got to sit at the soundboard, and she watched the lights and saw the guys onstage, and heard the roar of the crowd singing along to every song. And finally, she understood. She leaned in close and said, "I get it, Dad. *This* is what you used to do."

"Exactly," I said. "Exactly."

I'm a lucky guy. I've gotten to spend my whole life rocking. Here's hoping you can too.

Verse

Just because you work in a corporate environment doesn't mean you have to work in a button-down fashion. There are plenty of ways to shatter the corporate stereotype, starting with a more effective, less passive means of communication.

Chorus

Everyone wants more effective communication, but nobody's quite sure how to go about achieving it—not a surprise since communication involves at least two people, both of whom may have very different ideas about how to get messages across effectively. So as a team, consult on the best means of communication; what works for you may not work as well for your teammates. Listen and learn.

Solo

It's time to rock. Take the first steps toward kicking up your career to a higher level. How you do it is up to you, but what matters is that you try.

Encore
A Camp Jam
Crash Course

Involving people in a new enterprise and taking them out of their comfort zone can be an amazingly rewarding way to see how they handle pressure. Dangling someone off a cliff or pushing the person out of an airplane can put the pressure on him or her very quickly, but we tend to prefer a somewhat lower-risk environment. Through Camp Jam Inc., we've taught thousands of employees and executives how to rock. Here are some lessons we've learned along the way.

Growing into Your Role

Sports are always an effective team-building exercise; that's why the group of players on the field or the court is called a "team." But I prefer to think of a band as the most effective template for learning how to work together. Think of it this way: when you're in a band, you count to four and the "game" (a.k.a. the song) begins.

Your particular "game" may be only four or five minutes, but if anyone on the team "drops the ball" (fails to hold up their end, hits a wrong note, comes in too early or too late), the entire song is a waste, and the entire team is a failure. Rarely in sports does it all come down to a single play; in music, every beat is critical. Being in a band is like being part of the ultimate team; the collaboration, group creativity, and interdependence of making music together take the concept of teamwork to a different level. No matter how many musicians are in a band, it's the one sound created by many that is the goal, and that end result ultimately determines your success.

For a Camp Jam Inc. session, we break employees into "bands," dividing them up into groups of five or six without regard to prior musical experience. The guy who plays saxophone in an after-hours club goes right in with a new bandmate who's never once touched a guitar; the woman who had piano lessons all through elementary school may be paired up with a colleague who has never sung anywhere outside the shower.

Like the kids, the adults are excited, eager to get going on this new venture. (It sure beats sitting in a hotel ballroom watching yet another PowerPoint presentation any day of the week.) However, unlike the kids, the adults are often so nervous they can hardly speak. They make awkward jokes, wiggle the guitars in classic rock star style, and generally wait for the Camp Jam Inc. counselors—established musicians, all—to give them any kind of direction of what to do.

Where the kids often don't have a care in the world—or they don't know enough to be scared—the adults feel that they have something at stake. They realize that in three or four hours, they're going to be onstage in front of their friends, their peers, their employers, and they *really* don't want to screw that up.

There's an important element for managers to consider here. The longer someone has been in a comfortable environment, the worse this person will adapt to change and the longer the adjustment period will be. So think carefully about how to implement drastic changes, and consider whether less drastic changes are truly necessary. (Do you really need to switch coffee brands in the break room? Is a new expense-reporting system going to cause more trouble than it avoids?)

In our case, if our new musicians had been forced to take the stage after ten minutes—or even two hours—with their instruments, the results would have made yowling cats sound like opera. But with enough preparation and enough time to get comfortable in their new roles as rock stars, something amazing happens to our brand-new musicians: they start to see how they might just be able to pull this off.

With rock stars, it's (almost) all about attitude. Sid Vicious of the Sex Pistols probably had less musical talent than most of the people who visit our Camp Jam Inc. sessions. But he had attitude in truckloads that could carry him a long way with an audience.

Note, however, that I said it's *almost* all about attitude. A bit of musical ability is necessary for anyone to feel confident enough to get onstage, just as a few flying lessons are necessary for anyone to feel comfortable behind the controls of a plane. Fortunately, we've all had musicianship instilled in us since preschool, so getting onstage isn't as big a leap as, say, getting behind the controls of a jumbo jet in flight would be. It's that inherent musicianship that we seek out and build on during our sessions. Anyone can count to four, and that's the basis of all the songs we perform. Anyone can tap out a consistent rhythm, and that's the foundation of all the work on guitar and drums. Once the Camp Jam Inc. participants understand that, playing "Woolly Bully" or "Twist and Shout" onstage doesn't seem so daunting.

So once we teach everyone the basic elements of their various songs—in some cases, we have to show people which end of the guitar to hold, which is fine—we can start bringing them along the path that I've discussed in previous chapters, moving from individual musicianship to band interaction. They focus on learning their individual part, and once they've got that nailed, they focus on listening to one another and helping each other along.

Of course, they're doing it in hours rather than years, but then, they're doing a single song, not a career.

What's really fascinating to see is how the participants' personas grow as their confidence increases. Some people may start out clutching the guitar like a life preserver, but by the time they're onstage, they're flinging their arms in giant circles, Pete Townshend style, and duck-walking or high-stepping across the stage. A singer might start out so scared behind the microphone that she can't even look at the audience, but by showtime, she's shaking and shimmying as if she'd just stepped off the bus from Motown. Those finishing moves are an important element of any stage show—who wants to see a rock band standing still, for heaven's sake?—but until you've learned the basics of musicianship, your finishing moves are just clowning around.

The moral here is obvious. Having a destination in mind—in this case, playing onstage in four hours—is a powerful motivator. But having the confidence to know it's within your ability to reach that destination takes away much of the fear and self-doubt.

From the Mouths (and Guitars) of Babes

It's not just the adults who undergo a transformation. Undoubtedly you know about Robert Fulghum's book *Everything I Need to Know, I Learned in*

Kindergarten. Our version would run something like this: *Everything I Need to Know, I Learned from My First Rock Band.* Long before videos and recording contracts, long before multiplatinum hits and sold-out stadiums, there is the band. And the band is good.

Another element of Camp Jam is bringing music to kids through week-long summer camps. At the Camp Jam weeks, we bring together kids who have never met each other and in many cases have very little experience with their chosen instruments. We divide them into "bands," each with a combination of guitarists, bassists, drummers, singers, and perhaps a keyboard player or other instrumentalist.

Without exception, what we see develop every time is a study in human behavior, and if you pay close attention, you can see exactly how this can apply to a business setting.

When these kids get together, there's always someone who asserts himself or herself as a leader. Sometimes it's the one who wants to be the singer; sometimes it's a guitarist. (Every so often, someone will emulate Don Henley of the Eagles and try to run the show from the drummer's seat.) The leader steps forward and takes our instruction, relays it to the team, and serves as the point person for all contact, discussion, and recommendations. We don't decide that; the band does, usually almost unconsciously.

Another role that almost immediately gets filled is that of front man (or front woman, to be inclusive). The front man is the face of the band—the singer who's belting forth tunes and giving the band its identity. Think Mick Jagger or Aerosmith's Steven Tyler. Sometimes the front man and the leader are one and the same, as with U2's Bono; sometimes the front man is the mouthpiece for the leader, as with The Who. And sometimes the front man is just half of the leadership team, combining ideas and vision with one specific bandmate to reach higher ground—again, the Rolling Stones and Aerosmith.

But as we've seen many times throughout the book, a band can't work when it's full of front men. You need the role players, the team players, and we see that in our camps. Some kids don't have the desire or the charisma to stand in front of a band and dictate direction or stand in front of an audience and call out, "Here we are, world!" What these kids do have, however, is a willingness to go along and get along, to lay down the rock-solid foundation of the band.

You can always find yourself a flashy guitarist who will spin solo after solo and revel in the audience's applause. But a drummer or bass player you can set your watch to and rely on day after day, week after week, year after year is like gold, and you hold on to these people with both hands.

Observing kids in action as they form a band gives us a unique opportunity to see how the best bands come together. Why? Because when you're a teenager, your entire world is all about you, you, you. Maybe your significant other plays some part in your life; certainly you want your parents around as infrequently as possible. But for the most part, as any teenager (or former teenager) can tell you, your entire life is devoted entirely to satisfying whatever urge hits you at the moment. And that is why bands are so important to these kids. In a band, it's not about you; it's about the greater good. You want to do a solo project, great, but that's not what we're trying to do in Camp Jam! You park your ego and you join a band, and it's amazing how quickly things snap into place with these kids.

And as a result, we can see which group these kids are going to fit into from the moment they arrive at our camps. We can tell by the way a kid walks in the room, the way he talks with other campers, the way she stands or holds his instrument where he belongs or which band she'll help the most.

Here's a story about that kind of leadership from our days at Camp Jam. One morning as we were preparing for the day's lessons, a camper came over and spoke to us in that uncertain voice that told me he wasn't sure he was doing the right thing.

"My mom thinks I need to be in a better band," he said.

"Really," I replied. "Why does your mom think you need to be in a better band? Because you're the best musician in the band?"

"Yeah, I guess," he said. Which was true. He was definitely the most accomplished musician in his group.

"Let's look at this another way," I said. "Instead of you jumping ship on these guys, maybe you can bring them up to your level. Maybe you can be their leader. You can be the guy to get them to play better, to teach them how to play the music the way it ought to be played."

He was quiet for a moment, and slowly nodded. "You know, I never thought of it that way," he said. "That's what I'm going to do."

And as it turned out, the kid was a phenomenal musician, and before long, he'd inspired his band to phenomenal levels alongside him.

You can use these same ideas with newcomers to your organization, particularly if you have more than one arriving at once—a newly hired sales team, say, or a new crop of interns. Observing how they position themselves, how they work to fit into or mold their teams can help you guide them to the proper location within your organization.

Keep this in mind: the best bands are created not just by listening to what they play but observing how they play it.

Listen to a New Song Every Day

You're never done learning music. There's a grand myth that garage bands have "three chords and a dream," but only people who have never played in a band believe that music could stop at three chords. Mathematically, the possibilities for notes and chord combinations run into the billions, perhaps even trillions. But creatively, there is no limit. None whatsoever.

Look at it this way. You can know every song in the Bruce Springsteen songbook. You can figure out every tune Keith Richards or the Edge ever wrote. You can develop your ear to the point that you can pick out songs by hearing them on the radio. You can do all this, and you're only one step along your journey. Why? I'll give you four reasons, and then I'll tell you how they can apply to you, even if you don't know which end of a guitar to play:

- *You can learn to play what you already know better.* Sure, you can tear off the opening notes of "Purple Haze" or pound out the opening chords of "Smells Like Teen Spirit." But record your version of it and play it back; it'll sound as strange and awkward to you as hearing a recording of your own voice. Smooth it out, open it up, and release your inner Jimi!
- *You can learn the new music.* Every five years, somebody comes along to proclaim that rock 'n' roll (or hip-hop, or pop, or electronica, or whatever other genre you like) is dead, over, played out. And every six years, a brand-new band comes along resurrecting that genre from the "dead." Bob Dylan inspired Bruce Springsteen, who inspires today's The Hold Steady. The Rolling Stones inspired Guns 'n' Roses, who inspire today's The White Stripes. It's a lineage of music stretching nearly fifty years now, and it's not stopping any time soon, no matter what the critics say.
- *You can learn a new instrument.* So you can wow the neighborhood with your guitar skills, fingers flying through all the familiar songs and solos. Or maybe you've got the kind of voice that makes people nod in satisfaction at a karaoke night. You've mastered your instrument.

How about branching out? Learn to pick out some holiday tunes on the piano. Learn the basics of rhythm and fills on the drums. It's like learning a new language: the first one's tough; the second, not so much.

• *You can begin writing your own songs.* Here's where things begin to take off. When you stop imitating and start creating, that's where true nirvana lies, and I'm not talking about the band.

All of this advice is wonderful if you're looking to form a garage band, but you can obviously see that it applies equally well if you're looking at a third straight quarter of stagnant numbers. You can improve efficiencies in your own operations, or you can look across industries to see how others are meeting the same challenges in different ways. You can learn a new skill; if you're the desk-bound type, say, perhaps you could brush up on your public speaking and sales abilities. Or you can strike out on your own entirely, spearheading your own initiatives and wandering into that dark uncharted territory.

You don't know what you'll find if you venture out on that creative limb. But you know exactly what's in store if you stick with those same three chords.

We'd like to leave you with some thoughts that we've compiled over our careers, both together and separately, on how rock 'n' roll and business aren't very different after all. You learned three Rs in school; now you're about to learn five in rock music.

The 5 Rs of Rock and Business

Realize

When a band starts a new record, developing a unique vision for the product is top priority. A successful group will have a cohesive sound, look, and performance for every new album. The band must identify its audience and make sure the new product will serve that audience. As song ideas come together, every member of the group must feel involved in the creative process. All of these concepts must come together to form a direction that the entire group believes in and can get behind. Similarly, your team has to have in mind its vision, its goal, and its audience before diving deep into your project. Planning doesn't necessarily equal success, but lack of planning always results in failure.

Rehearse

As the band rehearses material for the upcoming recording sessions and tour, their most important tools are their eyes and ears. Every member must know when to be a participant and when to be an observer. Every detail of the music must be scrutinized and arranged perfectly. In truly great bands, the whole is greater than the sum of the parts. The music they create together, through collaboration and close listening, far surpasses anything they could accomplish on their own. Likewise, you and your team need to prep for every possible engagement, understanding the intricacies of your industry, your engagement, and your individual duties. Know your job back and forth, and you'll be better able to weather the surprises.

Record

Studio time costs a lot of money, so all band members must come to the recording sessions prepared to perform when their turn comes. Band members also must be flexible, because the parts that sounded great in rehearsal might not sound as good when recorded. Band members must shed their egos for the good of the product. Not everyone's instrument can be the loudest one on the record. Although everyone in the band might not be a virtuoso, the unique interaction of the team forms the group's unique sound. In the same way, your group has to understand how to function most effectively, with both dynamic and restrained personalities adding something to the mix. This isn't a solo product; you're a team, and every member needs to be engaged every step of the way.

Recap

After the album has been recorded, the band circles back to ask itself: Does this album accomplish what we set out to do? Will it reach our target audience? At this point, even the smallest details, like the final mix of the single or the picture chosen for the album cover, can have a profound effect on the success of the project. The marketing, rehearsal, and other preparations being made at this stage lay the groundwork for a successful tour. For businesses, this is the calm before the storm: your plans are in place, and you're waiting to see how the marketplace reacts. Will you be a success? Will you fail spectacularly? Whichever happens, you're prepared.

Rock!

After all of the preparation in rehearsals and in the studio, a band takes its product to the marketplace in the form of a tour. This is where the records and T-shirts are sold, and the money is made. Onstage, each member needs to know when to step into the spotlight and when to allow his or her bandmates to shine. During the tour, videos of performance are reviewed to fine-tune the show. Bands can't ever get complacent, because a hundred other bands are working hard to take that place at the top. And so are your competitors if you let them. Assess your position, take an honest inventory of your strengths and weaknesses, and reallocate time and resources as necessary. Always look forward, but never forget to step back and think about how you're going to get there. And don't be afraid to be loud!

Business is, quite simply, a battle of the bands. There are hundreds of bands out there that sound just like you, hundreds of businesses making products similar to yours. In this competitive environment, all of your band members have to be playing the same song in the same key. You need team members who know not only how to play the right notes, but also where to play those notes in the context of the music going on around them.

Here ends the lesson. Now get out there and rock!

The Authors

Jeff Carlisi was one of the founding members of 38 Special and cowrote many of its biggest hits, including "Second Chance," "Caught Up in You," and "Hold On Loosely." While Jeff was a member of 38 Special, the band sold over 14 million records and enjoyed worldwide popular and critical acclaim. He left the band in 1997. Since then, he has formed the band Big People, which has included members of the Cars and Ted Nugent's and Billy Joel's regular bands. Jeff is one of the cofounders of Camp Jam Inc., where he is training the next generation of rock musicians, and also plays in the Rock & Roll Hall of Fame's house band.

Dan Lipson has years of experience starting and running profitable companies. Before his involvement with Camp Jam, Dan served as president of Leading Edge

Promotions (now known as Strike Ten), a marketing firm. He has also served as CEO of Causelink.com, an Internet auction site for nonprofit fundraising, and founded ExL Corp., a sports catalogue and promotions company that is now a division of QVC. He began his career at ESPN, where he developed and produced *NASCAR Shop Talk*, the first transactional TV series on a national entertainment network.

In 2004, Jeff and Dan founded Camp Jam Inc. (www.campjam.com), a collection of rock 'n' roll music programs designed to educate and inspire. Camp Jam's offerings include rock 'n' roll camps for both adults and children in fifteen cities, corporate team-building exercises, and Camp Jam's Ultimate Rock 'n' Roll Getaway, a weekend rock music camp for adults. Camp Jam is the most comprehensive grouping of rock programs in America, and those programs have boasted attendance from musicians all over the world. Since Camp Jam's founding, the camp and its founders have appeared on the *NBC Nightly News, Good Morning America, CNN, CNN Headline News,* and other programs and in national publications including *Time, People, Woman's Day,* and a range of in-flight and city-specific magazines.

Jay Busbee is an editor at Yahoo! Sports, a contributing editor at *Atlanta* magazine, and a regular contributor to many other print and online outlets. A graduate of the College of William and Mary, with an M.F.A. from the University of Memphis, he has published more than a thousand articles in national magazines and newspapers, including *USA Today,* the *Washington Post,* ESPN.com, and Esquire.com.

Index

Printed and bound by CPI Group (UK) Ltd, Croydon, CR0 4YY

13/04/2025

14656498-0002